轻松学语音

Easy English Phonetics

主　编　黄春丽
副主编　康　丽　黄飞燕
编　者　李秋方　崔永杰　王琳琳

河南大学出版社
HENAN UNIVERSITY PRESS
·郑州·

图书在版编目（CIP）数据

轻松学语音 / 黄春丽主编. -- 郑州：河南大学出版社，2017.6
（2018.9 重印）
　ISBN 978-7-5649-2966-4

　Ⅰ.①轻… Ⅱ.①黄… Ⅲ.①英语—语音—自学参考资料
Ⅳ.① H311

中国版本图书馆 CIP 数据核字 (2017) 第 165957 号

责任编辑	林方丽
责任校对	陈　冲
封面设计	郭　灿
出　　版	河南大学出版社
	地址：郑州市郑东新区商务外环中华大厦 2401 号
	邮编：450046
	电话：0371-86059701（营销部）
	网址：www.hupress.com
排　　版	河南大学出版社
印　　刷	辉县市伟业印务有限公司
版　　次	2017 年 8 月第 1 版
印　　次	2018 年 9 月第 2 次印刷
开　　本	787mm×1092mm　1/16
印　　张	6.25
字　　数	115 千字
定　　价	24.00 元

（本书如有印装质量问题，请与河南大学出版社营销部联系调换）

前　　言

语音在英语学习过程中占据着非常重要的地位。学好语音有助于学习者提高听力和口语表达能力，还能帮助学习者快速入门，有效拼读、记忆、掌握单词，从而激发他们的英语学习兴趣，培养英语学习信心。

我国学生在初学英语时，由于学校缺乏简单、有趣、实用的语音教材，教师又对语音的重要性认识不足，因此，语音学习往往是蜻蜓点水式的浅尝辄止，缺乏系统的学习。这就造成英语初学者不能有效利用语音知识，错过了初学英语时快速入门的良机。后期的英语学习又多重在语法、口语、听力、阅读、写作等方面，缺少对语音知识的系统复习和巩固。这样的英语学习现状导致很多学生不能利用语音知识来快速有效地记忆单词，反复强化记忆单词的效果并不尽如人意，往往事倍功半，挫伤学习的积极性。

本书旨在使英语学习者通过对语音的学习快速入门，有效掌握单词，激发学习兴趣，培养学习信心。本书借鉴了马承老师的语音教学法，充分利用了迁移规律，借助汉语拼音和学生已有知识，将音标、单词、句子、对话（短文）四者有机结合。本书以简易、风趣、实用为三大准则，收录了英语绕口令、歌谣、游戏、常用口语、格言谚语等内容。各部分内容互为补充，使英语语音学习轻松、有趣、快速、有效。

在编写本书的过程中，我们参考、引用、借鉴了国内同行的研究成果，在此表示衷心的感谢！由于编者水平有限，书中难免有疏漏、不当之处，恳请各位读者指正。

编者

2017年2月

目录 Contents

前言 1
Unit 1　英语字母 1
Unit 2　元音字母 Aa 的短音 6
Unit 3　元音字母 Ee 的短音 11
Unit 4　元音字母 Ii 的短音 15
Unit 5　元音字母 Oo 的短音 19
Unit 6　元音字母 Uu 的短音 23
Unit 7　短音音标 /ʊ/ /ə/ 27
Unit 8　元音字母的名称音 31
Unit 9　长音音标 /iː/ /ɔː/ /ɜː/ /uː/ /ɑː/ 36
Unit 10　双元音 /aɪ/ /aʊ/ /eɪ/ /əʊ/ 41
Unit 11　双元音 /ɪə/ /eə/ /ɔɪ/ /ʊə/ 45
Unit 12　辅音音标 /θ/ /ð/ /j/ /ŋ/ 50
Unit 13　辅音音标 /ʃ/ /ʒ/ /tʃ/ /dʒ/ 55
Unit 14　辅音音标 /tr/ /dr/ /ts/ /dz/ 60
Unit 15　语音知识 65
附录一：语音小常识 70
附录二：常见字母 (组合) 的发音 75
附录三：常用口语 80
附录四：格言谚语 85
附录五：自我检测 90
参考文献 91

Unit 1　英语字母

Alphabet

Aa	Bb	Cc	Dd	Ee	Ff	Gg
Hh	Ii	Jj	Kk	Ll	Mm	Nn
Oo	Pp	Qq		Rr	Ss	Tt
Uu	Vv	Ww		Xx	Yy	Zz

26 个字母包括 5 个元音字母和 21 个辅音字母。

元音字母：　Aa　　Ee　　Ii　　Oo　　Uu

辅音字母：　Bb　　Cc　　Dd　　Ff　　Gg　　Hh　　Jj
　　　　　　　Kk　　Ll　　Mm　　Nn　　Pp　　Qq　　Rr
　　　　　　　Ss　　Tt　　Vv　　Ww　　Xx　　Yy　　Zz

手写体

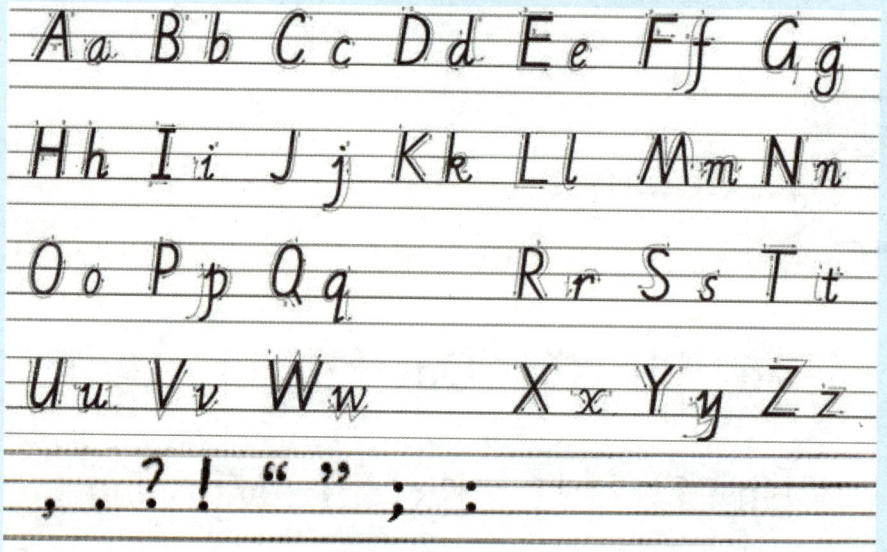

书写口诀：

字母书写有规则，右倾 10° 正适宜。

大写都在上两格，上不顶天下立地。

有头要占上两格，b d h k l t，有尾拖到下两格，g p q y，

无头无尾在中间，a c e m n o，加上 r s u v w x z，

i，j 不一般，一格半来两格半，小 f 最特别，三格全部都要占。

仔细看来认真练，养成书写好习惯。

附注：汉语句号"。"是小圆圈，而英语句号"."是实心点。书写标点符号时，英语的逗号","和句号"."要紧贴在第三线的上方，不要写在第二格的中间。

Unit 1 英语字母

Abbreviations

A.M. 上午	**ATM** 自动取款机	**BBC** 英国广播公司
CCTV 中央电视台	**CEO** 首席执行官	**DNA** 脱氧核糖核酸
FBI （美国）联邦调查局	**GPS** 全球定位系统	**ID Card** 身份证
IELTS 雅思	**IQ** 智商	**IT** 信息技术
NBA 美国职业篮球联赛	**P.M.** 下午	**PRC** 中华人民共和国
SOS 紧急求救信号	**TOEFL** 托福	**UFO** 不明飞行物
UK 英国	**UN** 联合国	**USA** 美国
VIP 贵宾	**VOA** 美国之音	**WTO** 世界贸易组织

轻松学语音

A Rhyme: Four Seasons

Spring is gay with flowers and song.

Summer is hot and the days are long.

Autumn is rich with fruit and grain.

Winter brings snow and the New Year again.

译文：春季欢乐百花香，夏季炎热白昼长，
　　　　秋季丰收粮和果，冬季飞雪迎新忙。

A Song: Bingo

There was a farmer who had a dog.

And Bingo was his name-O!

B-I-N-G-O! B-I-N-G-O! B-I-N-G-O!

And Bingo was his name-O!

译文：有一个农夫有一只狗，宾果是它的名字。

Unit 1 英语字母

Fun Time

1. Which letter is a drink?
2. Which letter is an animal?
3. Which letter is a kind of vegetable?
4. Which letter is a question?
5. Which letter is a part of your face?
6. Draw a picture from A to Z.

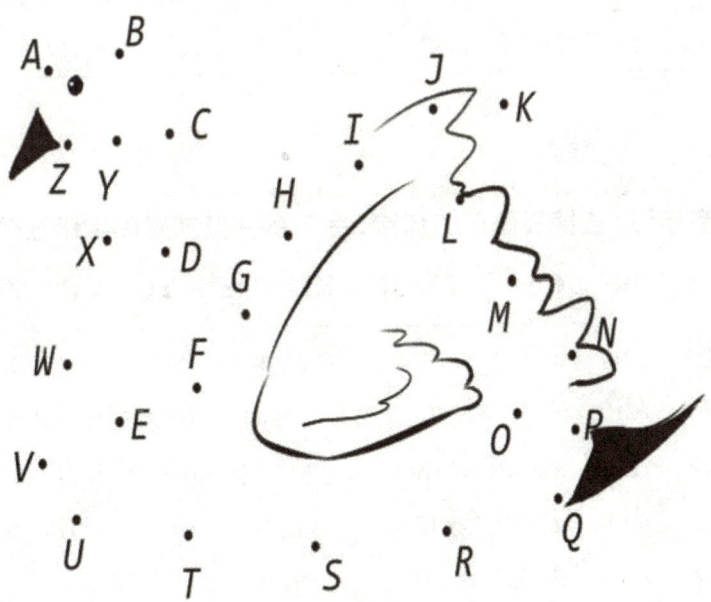

轻松学语音

Unit 2 元音字母 Aa 的短音

Learn to Read

掐头法学读音

读以下辅音字母，去掉其第一个音素，余下的音素就是该字母在单词中的读音。

    Ff Ll Mm Nn Ss Xx

Ff	/ef/	去 /e/	余 /f/	**Ll**	/el/	去 /e/	余 /l/
Mm	/em/	去 /e/	余 /m/	**Nn**	/en/	去 /e/	余 /n/
Ss	/es/	去 /e/	余 /s/	**Xx**	/eks/	去 /e/	余 /ks/

去尾法学读音

读以下辅音字母，去掉其尾部的音素，余下的音素就是该字母在单词中的读音。

   Bb Cc Dd Jj Kk Pp Tt Vv Zz

Bb	/biː/	去 /iː/	余 /b/	**Cc**	/siː/	去 /iː/	余 /s/
Dd	/diː/	去 /iː/	余 /d/	**Jj**	/dʒeɪ/	去 /eɪ/	余 /dʒ/
Kk	/keɪ/	去 /eɪ/	余 /k/	**Pp**	/piː/	去 /iː/	余 /p/
Tt	/tiː/	去 /iː/	余 /t/	**Vv**	/viː/	去 /iː/	余 /v/
Zz	/ziː/	去 /iː/	余 /z/				

注：Cc 还有另外一个常发的音 /k/。

Unit 2　元音字母 Aa 的短音

元音字母 Aa →/æ/

fat　　　　cat　　　　bag
胖的　　　　猫　　　　包

A fat cat is in a bag.

map　　　　man　　　　hand
地图　　　　男人　　　　手

A map is in a man's hand.

Dialogue 1

Sam: You look sad. What happened?

Ann: I lost my cat and my handbag.

Sam: It's too bad. But the cat will be back.

Ann: Who knows? I can't stand this fact.

Dialogue 2

Ann: Do you like apples?

Sam: Yeah! I like apples. What about you?

Ann: Me, too. An apple a day keeps the doctor away.

Sam: Sure. By the way, do you have a plan for this Saturday?

Ann: I plan to visit my grandma.

轻松学语音

Tongue Twisters

1. Cat, cat, catch that fat rat!
2. Jack is glad that you are back.
3. A cat has a fat dad with a big hat. A man has a fat hand with a ham.
4. A fat man sat on the black cat and the black cat was flat, for the man was mad.
5. Can you can a can as a canner can can a can?
6. Canners can can what they can can but cannot can things that can't be canned.

译文: 5. 你能够像罐头工人一样装罐头吗？6. 罐头工人能够把他们能做成罐头的东西制成罐头，但是不能把无法制成罐头的东西制成罐头。

A Rhyme: A Cap on a Cat

A cap on a cat. A cap on a dog.

A cap on a rabbit. A cap on a frog.

Rain, snow or sun, caps are always fun.

译文: 帽子小猫戴，帽子小狗爱。帽子兔子戴，帽子青蛙爱。
雨雪艳阳日，戴帽美滋滋。

Unit 2　元音字母 Aa 的短音

A Song: Mary Had a Little Lamb

Mary had a little lamb,
Little lamb, little lamb,
Mary had a little lamb,
Its fleece was white as snow.

And everywhere that Mary went,
Mary went, Mary went,
Everywhere that Mary went,
The lamb was sure to go.

译文：玛丽有只小羊羔，
浑身雪白卷卷毛。

无论玛丽去哪里，
哪里就有小羊羔。

Fun Time

1: Reasonable Answer

Tom: Dad, why do fish live in water?
Dad: Because cats cannot swim.

合理的回答

汤姆：爸爸，为什么鱼在水里生活？
爸爸：因为猫不会游泳。

9

轻松学语音

2: Close Your Eyes and Write

Ted: Dad, can you close your eyes and write down your name?

Dad: Of course I can.

Ted: Then please do that here.

Dad: What is this?

Ted: My school report, Dad.

闭上你的眼睛写

泰德： 爸爸，你能闭上眼睛写下你的名字吗？

爸爸： 当然。

泰德： 那就请你在这里写吧。

爸爸： 这是什么？

泰德： 我的成绩报告单。

3: Watering Flowers

Mum: What are you doing there, Mary?

Mary: I'm watering the flowers.

Mum: But it's raining.

Mary: It doesn't matter, Mum. I have an umbrella.

浇花

妈妈： 玛丽，你在那里干什么？

玛丽： 给花浇水。

妈妈： 可是天在下雨呀。

玛丽： 不要紧，妈妈，我打着伞呢。

Unit 3　元音字母 Ee 的短音

Learn to Read

对比法学读音

英语辅音字母 g, h, r, w, y 在英语单词中的发音与汉语拼音 g, h, r, w, y 的读音相似。比较两者的区别。

汉语拼音　g,　h,　r,　w,　y
英语发音　/g/ /h/ /r/ /w/ /j/

元音字母 Ee →/e/

ten	pen	desk
十	钢笔	书桌

Ten pens are on a desk.

pet	red	bed
宠物	红色的	床

My pet is on the red bed.

11

 轻松学语音

Dialogue 1

Ted: You look pretty in this dress.

Betty: Thanks. I'm glad to hear that.

Ted: Really. You look much better in red.

Betty: Do I? In fact, I like to be dressed in yellow.

Ted: Oh no! You look better in red!

Dialogue 2

Ted: I'm glad to see you again, Betty.

Betty: I'm glad to see you, too, Ted.

Ted: What's that in your hand?

Betty: Can you guess what…

Ted: It looks like a…

Betty: Look! This is a new pen.

Ted: A new pen? It looks very pretty.

Tongue Twisters

1. All is well that ends well.

2. East or west, home is best.

3. Is Ellen's dress red or yellow?

4. Better to do well than to say well.

5. Ted is getting ready for the next lesson.

6. Ben sent Helen ten hens and Helen sent Ben ten pens.

译文： 1. 结果好就一切都好。 2. 东好西好，不如家好。 4. 说得好不如做得好。

Unit 3　元音字母 Ee 的短音

A Rhyme: Good, Better, Best

Good, better, best,

Never let it rest.

Till good is better,

And better, best.

译文：好上加好求更好，

永不停步向前跑。

做到好后要更好，

最好又把更好超。

A Song: Ten Little Indian Boys

One little, two little, three little Indians.

Four little, five little, six little Indians.

Seven little, eight little, nine little Indians.

Ten little Indian boys.

Ten little, nine little, eight little Indians.

Seven little, six little, five little Indians.

Four little, three little, two little Indians.

One little Indian boy.

轻松学语音

Fun Time: Puzzle

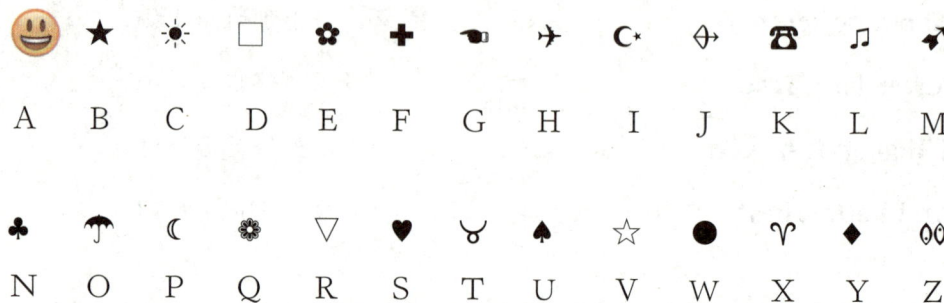

Example:

☪ ✈ 😀 ☆ ❀ 😀 □ ▽ ❀ 😀 ➹

= I have a dream.

1. ● ✈ 😀 ♉ ➹ 😀 ♣ ☀ 😀 ♣ ☂ ♉ ♪ ☪ ☆ ❀ ☪ ♣ 😀 ✈ ☂ ♠ ❀

=

2. ● ✈ 😀 ♉ ✈ 😀 ♥ 😀 ♉ ☂ ♣ 🕻 ❀ ★ ♣ ☀ 😀 ♣ ☂ ♉ 😀 ♪ 🕻

=

Unit 4 元音字母 Ii 的短音

Learn to Read

字母组合记忆法

字母组合 ck, ch, sh 在英语中很常见，它们与汉语拼音中的声母 k, ch, sh 发音接近，注意两者的不同。

字母组合	ck	ch	sh
	black	rich	fish
汉语拼音	k（克）	ch（吃）	sh（狮）

元音字母 Ii → /ɪ/

big	pig	ship
大的	猪	轮船

A big pig is on a ship.

Bill	swim	fish
比尔	游泳	鱼

Bill can swim like a fish.

Dialogue

Bill: Who is the girl in the middle?

Dick: This is Mary, my little sister.

Bill: How old is she?

Dick: She's six. I often play with her at home.

Bill: She's so cute.

Passage

　　My little sister, Lily, is six. She lives in a big city with Nancy. Nancy is a rich lady. She has six kids. They make her very busy. She works in a ticket office. Nancy is happy, because her family are happy. She often takes the kids to visit her office. The kids love Nancy, and Nancy loves them, too.

Tongue Twisters

1. Sixty-six sick chicks.
2. Will will not write a real will.
3. I wish you were a fish in my dish.
4. —Will you sit still, Bill? —I'll sit as still as a hill.
5. Bill isn't as thin as Tim. Dick isn't as fat as Jim. They do the same thing. The same house they live in.
6. I wish to wish the wish you wish to wish, but if you wish the wish the witch wishes, I won't wish the wish you wish to wish.

译文： 2. 威尔不会写真实的遗嘱。4. —比尔，你坐着别动好吗？—我会坐着像山一样岿然不动。6. 我希望梦想着你梦想中的梦想，但是如果你梦想着女巫的梦想，我就不想梦想着你梦想中的梦想。

Unit 4　元音字母 Ii 的短音

A Rhyme: Silly Billy

Silly Billy! Silly Billy!

Why is Silly Billy silly?

Why does Silly Billy love Lily?

Silly Billy isn't silly.

译文：傻比利！傻比利！

为什么傻比利傻？

为什么傻比利爱莉莉？

傻比利并不傻。

A Song: Twinkle, Twinkle, Little Star

Twinkle, twinkle, little star,

How I wonder what you are!

Up above the world so high,

Like a diamond in the sky.

译文：一闪一闪小星星，星光神秘亮晶晶，
高高挂在夜空中，宝石一样放光明。

Fun Time: A or An?

___ baby   ___ elephant   ___ shirt   ___ orange

___ egg   ___ horse   ___ knife   ___ hour

___ apple   ___ uncle   ___ hat   ___ man

___ ear   ___ engineer   ___ hand   ___ eye

___ European   ___ university   ___ door   ___ cup

___ useful book   ___ ugly dog   ___ old man

___ 1-year-old girl   ___ 11-year-old boy   ___ honest boy

Unit 5　元音字母 Oo 的短音

Learn to Read

辅音字母	b	p	m	f	d	t	n	l
音标符号	/b/	/p/	/m/	/f/	/d/	/t/	/n/	/l/
辅音字母	g	k	h	r	s	z	v	w
音标符号	/g/	/k/	/h/	/r/	/s/	/z/	/v/	/w/

元音字母 Oo →/ɒ/

clock　　　　on　　　　box
钟表　　　在……上面　　盒子

A clock is on a box.

hot　　　　dog　　　　shop
热的　　　　狗　　　　商店

It is a hot dog shop.

Dialogue 1

Bob: What's this in the box?

John: In the box? It's a clock.

Bob: What's that in the bottle?

John: In the bottle? It's coffee.

Dialogue 2

Tom: Where is the doctor?

Molly: The doctor is in the room.

Tom: Where is the boss?

Molly: The boss is talking with the doctor.

Tongue Twisters

1. A fox in socks is on a box.
2. Thomas lost his office job.
3. Copy the song; it's not long.
4. Lost time is never found again.
5. They've gone to the coffee shop.
6. Dog, dog, my little dog, we can jog in the morning when it is not very hot.

译文：4. 时不再来。

Unit 5　元音字母 Oo 的短音

A Rhyme: A Cock

It's a cock,　　　　　　　　　译文：一只小公鸡，
Sitting on a rock,　　　　　　　　坐在石头上。
Wearing a sock,　　　　　　　　穿着一只袜，
And looking at a clock.　　　　　等着钟声响。

A Song: Old MacDonald Had a Farm

Old Macdonald had a farm, E-I-E-I-O!

And on this farm he had some ducks, E-I-E-I-O!

With a quack quack here, and a quack quack there.

Here a quack, there a quack, everywhere a quack quack.

Old Macdonald had a farm, E-I-E-I-O!

译文：老麦克唐纳有个农场，咿呀咿呀哟。
　　　农场里有些鸭，咿呀咿呀哟。
　　　这里嘎嘎，那里嘎嘎，
　　　到处都是嘎嘎叫。
　　　老麦克唐纳有个农场，咿呀咿呀哟。

轻松学语音

Fun Time

1. 从 ANDOGONEWHATHEYOU 中找出 17 个英语单词。

2. 单词接龙：apple—egg—get—ten—…

3. 游戏 doublets：两个长度相同的单词（比如 sit 和 cat），从 sit 开始，每次改变一个字母，变为另一个单词，直到变为 cat 为止，例如：sit—fit—fat—cat。请将 man 变为 bed。

4. 宾果 Bingo。

Draw nine squares on a piece of paper. Write numbers from one to nine in the squares.

1	7	4
8	3	9
2	5	6

Unit 6　元音字母 Uu 的短音

Learn to Read

元音字母 Uu →/ʌ/

fun	run	sun
有趣	跑	太阳

It is fun to run in the sun.

mum	lunch	bus
妈妈	午饭	公共汽车

Mum is out for lunch by bus.

Dialogue

Bob: Why are you in such a hurry?
John: Because I must hurry to catch the last bus.
Bob: Good luck to you!
John: Thank you! Have fun!

Passage

　　Ruskin comes from the country. She lives in London. Her husband is Frank. He sells brushes to make money. He also runs a club. It's a truck club. He runs it just for fun. They spend much of their time helping others in trouble.

轻松学语音

Summary

重读闭音节是以一个元音字母加一个或几个辅音字母结尾（元辅结构）的重读音节。在重读闭音节中，元音字母 a, e, i, o, u 不是发它本身的字母音，而是发短元音。

Aa	/æ/	man	bag	map	dad	cat	fat	hand
Ee	/e/	desk	pen	ten	red	best	egg	bed
Ii	/ɪ/	big	pig	ship	swim	fish	six	is
Oo	/ɒ/	box	on	not	hot	dog	shop	clock
Uu	/ʌ/	fun	sun	run	mum	bus	cup	must

Tongue Twisters

1. Bunny is a lovely funny girl.

2. I love my mother very much.

3. Mum, I want some duck meat!

4. Double bubble gum bubbles double.

5. My brother needs some money to buy some honey.

6. What fun! A plum bun. Yummy! I am not hungry! I can run in the sun!

译文： 4. 双重的泡泡糖能吹双重的泡泡。

Unit 6　元音字母 Uu 的短音

A Rhyme: Star Light, Star Bright

Star light, star bright,
First star I see tonight.
I wish I may, I wish I might,
Have the wish I wish tonight.

译文：星儿明，星儿亮，
今晚我看见初出的星星在闪光，
我希望我能够，
实现我今晚的愿望。

A Song: One, Two, Three, Four, Five

One, two, three, four, five,
Once I caught a fish alive.
Six, seven, eight, nine, ten,
Then I let it go again.
Why did you let it go?
Because it bit my finger so.
Which finger did it bite?
This little finger on the right.

译文：一二三四五，
我曾经活捉了一条鱼。
六七八九十，
然后我又把它放了。
你为什么放它走？
因为它咬了我的手指。
它咬的哪根手指？
右手的小指。

Fun Time

1: A Wet Plate

Customer: Waiter, the plate you gave me is wet.

Waiter: Oh, that's your soup, sir.

湿盘子

顾客：服务员，你给我的盘子是湿的。

服务员：哦，先生，那是你的汤。

2: Star and Moon

Father: What does the "0" mean on your test paper?

Son: I think it's a moon. The teacher ran out of stars.

星星和月亮

父亲：你考试卷上的"0"是什么意思？

儿子：我看那是月亮。老师的星星都用完了。

3: A Big Umbrella

Jim: I saw six men share one umbrella and none of them got wet.

Nick: Oh, that must be a very big umbrella.

Jim: No, it wasn't raining.

一把大伞

吉姆：我看见六个人合用一把大伞，却没有一个被淋湿。

尼克：哦，那伞一定很大。

吉姆：不，当时并没有下雨。

Unit 7　短音音标 /ʊ/ /ə/

Learn to Read

短元音　　/æ/　/e/　/ɪ/　/ɒ/　/ʌ/　/ʊ/　/ə/

/æ/	/fæt/	/kæt/	/bæɡ/	/mæn/	/hænd/
/e/	/ten/	/pen/	/desk/	/best/	/frend/
/ɪ/	/bɪɡ/	/pɪɡ/	/ʃɪp/	/swɪm/	/fɪʃ/
/ɒ/	/ɒn/	/klɒk/	/bɒks/	/hɒt/	/dɒɡ/
/ʌ/	/fʌn/	/sʌn/	/mʌst/	/bʌs/	/mʌm/
/ʊ/	/ɡʊd/	/bʊk/	/lʊk/	/tʊk/	/fʊt/
/ə/	/əˈhed/	/ˈdɒktə(r)/	/ˈkʌlə(r)/	/ˈwɔːtə(r)/	/ˈsɪstə(r)/

look　/lʊk/　　　good　/ɡʊd/　　　book　/bʊk/
　看　　　　　　　好的　　　　　　书

Look! It's a good book.

color　/ˈkʌlə(r)/　　sweater　/ˈswetə(r)/　　doctor　/ˈdɒktə(r)/
颜色　　　　　　　　毛衣　　　　　　　　　医生

What color is your sweater, doctor?

Summary

字母组合

oo →/ʊ/   b**oo**k 书   g**oo**d 好的   l**oo**k 看

er, or →/ə/   sist**er** 姐妹   wat**er** 水   doct**or** 医生

Dialogue

Ted: May I have a look at the book?

Betty: Sure. Here you are.

Ted: Oh, it's a very good book.

Betty: Yes. It's a very good cookbook.

Ted: Could you cook some food for us?

Betty: I'd love to.

Passage

Lora is eleven. She is a very clever girl. At school, she often makes her teacher happy with her good manners. After school, she often goes out with her classmates. Sometimes, they go to visit the nearby farmers. Sometimes, they go to buy books by famous writers. She likes writing letters to her friends. She also likes to collect pictures of famous men. She says that she enjoys looking at them.

Unit 7　短音音标 /ʊ/ /ə/

Tongue Twisters

1. A good book is a good friend.
2. You should take a good look at the book.
3. The teachers will get together tomorrow.
4. What do you call your father's mother's daughter's sister?
5. Mr. Cook said to a cook, "Look at this cookbook. It's very good." So the cook took the advice of Mr. Cook and bought the book.
6. How many cookies could a good cook cook, if a good cook could cook cookies? A good cook could cook as many cookies as a good cook who could cook cookies.

译文： 5. 库克先生对一名厨师说："看看这本烹饪书。它很不错。"因此厨师接受了库克先生的建议，买了那本书。6. 如果一个好的厨师能做小甜饼，那么他能做多少小甜饼呢？一个好的厨师能做出和其他会做小甜饼的好厨师一样多的小甜饼。

A Rhyme: Eeny, Meeny, Miny, Moe

Eeny, meeny, miny, moe,

Catch a tiger by the toe.

If he hollers, let him go,

Eeny, meeny, miny, moe.

注释： toe /təʊ/ 脚趾；足尖。holler /ˈhɒlə(r)/ 叫喊。Eeny, meeny, miny, moe 没有特殊含义，只是叽里咕噜念咒的咒语，相传来自远古凯尔特人祭祀神灵的用语。这首歌谣是儿童使用的瞎蒙选择手段，类似于汉语中的"点兵点将点到谁我就选谁"。还可以再加上 My mother told me to pick the very best one, and that is Y-O-U。

轻松学语音

A Song: Row, Row, Row Your Boat

Row, row, row your boat,　　　　　译文：划呀，划呀，划小船，
Gently down the stream.　　　　　　　　　 平稳地顺流而下。
Merrily, merrily, merrily, merrily,　　　　多么快乐，多么快乐，
Life is but a dream.　　　　　　　　　　　 生活就像一场梦。

Fun Time：Crossword（纵横字谜）

Unit 8　元音字母的名称音

Learn to Read

重读开音节是指以辅音字母 + 元音字母结尾（辅元结构）的音节或以元音字母 + 辅音字母 + 不发音的 e 结尾（元辅 e 结构）的重读音节。在重读开音节中，元音字母 a, e, i, o, u 分别发各自的名称音。

	Aa	Ee	Ii	Oo	Uu
闭音节	hat/hæt/	hen/hen/	his/hɪz/	not/nɒt/	us/ʌs/
开音节	hate/heɪt/	he/hi:/	hi/haɪ/	no/nəʊ/	use/ju:z/

name /neɪm/　　　　Jane /dʒeɪn/　　　　game /ɡeɪm/
　名字　　　　　　　　简　　　　　　　　　游戏

My name is Jane. Let's play a game.

we /wi:/　　　　　　he /hi:/　　　　　　me /mi:/
　我们　　　　　　　　他　　　　　　　　　我

We like him. They like me.

ride /raɪd/　　　　white /waɪt/　　　　bike /baɪk/
　骑　　　　　　　　白色的　　　　　　　自行车

Mike can ride a white bike.

so /səʊ/   **go** /gəʊ/   **home** /həʊm/
如此   去   家

It's so cold. Let's go home.

cube /kju:b/   **huge** /hju:dʒ/   **cute** /kju:t/
立方体   巨大的   可爱的

The Water Cube is very huge.

Dialogue

Mike: Who is that lady at the gate?

Dave: She is Jane. She comes from Rome.

Mike: What does she do?

Dave: She is a famous writer. She spends a lot of time writing.

Mike: Do you know her?

Dave: Yes, I'd like to introduce you to her.

Passage

    Mike likes riding his bike. But now he has a new car. He often drives his car to enjoy the wild life. Mike's wife likes to stay at home and make cakes. His daughter is nine. She is a brave girl. She likes to fly a kite in the blue sky. His son is five. Mike often takes them in his car to the wild. Last Sunday, they decided to go to the zoo. Due to the rain, they were late and the gate was closed. Do you know why the gate was closed when it was only nine o'clock?

Unit 8　元音字母的名称音

Tongue Twisters

1. Haste makes waste.

2. Don't go home alone.

3. My dog hopes to hide the bone at home.

4. Nine children are flying kites on the ice.

5. Please stay behind to taste the pie and the wine.

6. Dave with some cake goes out of the gate for a date.

译文：1. 欲速则不达。

Poems: Stray Birds （节选）

The bird wishes it were a cloud.　　　　　　　　鸟儿愿为一朵云。

The cloud wishes it were a bird.　　　　　　　　云儿愿为一只鸟。

If you shed tears when you miss the sun, you also miss the stars.
　　　　　　　如果你因错过太阳而流泪，那么你也将错过群星。

Let life be beautiful like summer flowers and death like autumn leaves.
　　　　　　　使生如夏花之绚烂，死如秋叶之静美。

I cannot choose the best. The best chooses me.
　　　　　　　我不能选择那最好的，是那最好的选择我。

（泰戈尔 Rabindranath Tagore, 1861~1941, 印度诗人，1913 年获得诺贝尔文学奖。）

轻松学语音

A Song: You Are My Sunshine

You are my sunshine, my only sunshine,

You make me happy when skies are gray.

You'll never know dear, how much I love you,

Please don't take my sunshine away.

The other night dear, as I lay sleeping,

I dreamed I held you in my arms.

When I awoke dear, I was mistaken,

So I hung my head and cried.

译文:

你就是我的阳光,我唯一的阳光 / 当天空乌云密布时你使我快乐 / 亲爱的,你不会知道我是多么爱你 / 请别带走我的阳光

亲爱的,又是一个晚上,我渐渐睡去 / 在梦境中我把你拥入怀中 / 可当我醒来,亲爱的,我错了 / 我垂下头开始哭泣

Fun Time

1: A Safe Lock

A man wanted to buy a lock. The shop assistant showed him some. The man took up one of them and asked, "Is this lock safe?"

"Sure," said the assistant, "even the key sometimes won't open it."

Unit 8 元音字母的名称音

保险锁

有一个人想买锁。店员给他看了一些。那人拿起一把锁,问:"这锁保险吗?"

"当然,"店员说,"有时候甚至用钥匙都打不开它。"

2: Who Will Hear It?

Mother: Oh, Tommy, what's wrong with your finger?

Tommy: I cut my finger.

Mother: But I didn't hear you cry this time.

Tommy: I didn't know you were at home.

谁会听见?

母亲:哦,汤米,你的手指怎么了?

汤米:我割破手指了。

母亲:可这次我没有听见你哭啊。

汤米:我不知道你在家。

3: You Are My Dad

Father: Come, Debbie, get out of bed.

Debbie: No!

Father: Don't you "no" me!

Debbie: Of course I know you! You're my dad!

你是我爹

父亲:黛比,快起床。

黛比:不!

父亲:你别对我说不!(你不认得我?!)

黛比:我当然认得你,你是我爹!

Unit 9 长音音标 /iː/ /ɔː/ /ɜː/ /uː/ /ɑː/

Learn to Read

长短元音					
短元音	/ɪ/	/ɒ/	/ə/	/ʊ/	/ʌ/
长元音	/iː/	/ɔː/	/ɜː/	/uː/	/ɑː/
/iː/	/biː/	/miː/	/siː/	/riːd/	/wiːk/
/ɔː/	/hɔːs/	/tɔːl/	/smɔːl/	/fɔː(r)/	/bɔːn/
/ɜː/	/gɜːl/	/skɜːt/	/nɜːs/	/bɜːd/	/ˈdɜːti/
/uː/	/ruːm/	/skuːl/	/bluː/	/muːn/	/tuː/
/ɑː/	/kɑː/	/pɑːk/	/glɑːs/	/ɑːsk/	/fɑːm/

eat /iːt/　　　meat /miːt/　　　week /wiːk/
　吃　　　　　　肉　　　　　　星期

We eat meat every week.

tall /tɔːl/　　　horse /hɔːs/　　　talk /tɔːk/
　高的　　　　　马　　　　　　谈话

Can the tall horse talk?

Unit 9 长音音标 /iː/ /ɔː/ /ɜː/ /uː/ /ɑː/

g**ir**l /gɜːl/　　　sk**ir**t /skɜːt/　　　d**ir**ty /ˈdɜːti/
女孩　　　　　　裙子　　　　　　　脏的

The girl's skirt is dirty.

bl**ue** /bluː/　　　m**oo**n /muːn/　　　t**oo** /tuː/
蓝色的　　　　　月亮　　　　　　　太

The blue moon is too big.

p**ar**k /pɑːk/　　　f**ar** /fɑː(r)/　　　f**ar**m /fɑːm/
公园　　　　　　远的　　　　　　　农场

The park is far from the farm.

Summary

字母组合

ea, ee → /iː/	sea 大海	see 看见	tea 茶
or, al → /ɔː/	small 小的	short 短的	talk 谈话
ir → /ɜː/	girl 女孩	shirt 衬衫	bird 小鸟
oo, ue → /uː/	blue 蓝色的	school 学校	cool 酷的
ar → /ɑː/	garden 花园	star 星星	park 公园

轻松学语音

Dialogue 1

Eve: Excuse me, how can I get to the park?

Carl: Go two blocks. Turn left. It's on First Street.

Eve: OK. Go two blocks. Turn left.

Carl: Right. It's on First Street. You can't miss it.

Eve: Thank you.

Dialogue 2

Peter: Who is this?

Eve: He's my brother, George.

Peter: Wow, he looks cool and smart. What does he like?

Eve: He likes sports. He often plays football with his friends after school.

Peter: Really? I like sports, too.

Tongue Twisters

1. First come, first served.
2. Trudy's dream has come true at last.
3. The nurses in skirts washed thirty dirty shirts.
4. George walked out of the courtyard with a saw.
5. I scream, you scream, and we all scream for ice cream!
6. Master Carter asked his class to play cards in the park.
7. I don't need your needles, they are needless to me, for the needing of needles is needless, you see.

译文: 1. 先到先得。7. 我不需要你的针，它们对我没用，因为你知道根本不需要针。

Unit 9 长音音标 /i:/ /ɔ:/ /ɜ:/ /u:/ /ɑ:/

A Rhyme: You Have One, I Have One

You have one, I have one,

Two little children see a big man.

You have two, I have two,

Four little children go to school.

You have three, I have three,

Six little children plant many trees.

You have four, I have four,

Eight little children stand at the door.

You have five, I have five,

Ten little children stand in a line.

A Song: The Farmer in the Dell

The farmer in the dell. The farmer in the dell.

Hi-ho, the derry-o… The farmer in the dell.

The farmer takes a wife. The farmer takes a wife.

Hi-ho, the derry-o…The farmer takes a wife.

The cheese stands alone. The cheese stands alone.

Hi-ho, the derry-o…The cheese stands alone.

※ child / dog / cat / rat / cheese

Fun Time: Frozen（冰雪奇缘）

Anna: Elsa. Psst! Elsa! Wake up! Wake up! Wake up!

Elsa: Anna, go back to sleep.

Anna: I just can't. The sky's awake, so I'm awake. So, we have to play.

Elsa: Go play by yourself.

Anna: Do you want to build a snowman? Come on, come on, come on, come on! Do the magic! Do the magic! Oh...

Elsa: Ready?

Anna: Uh-huh. This is amazing!

Elsa: Watch this! Hi, I'm Olaf and I like warm hugs.

Anna: I love you, Olaf. Tickle bumps!

Elsa: Hang on. Catch me!

Anna: Gotcha! Again!

Elsa: Wait! Slow down! Anna! Anna? Mama! Papa! You're okay, Anna. I got you.

Papa: Elsa, what have you done? This is getting out of hand!

Elsa: It was an accident. I'm sorry, Anna!

Mama: She's ice cold.

Papa: I know where we have to go.

Unit 10 双元音 /aɪ/ /aʊ/ /eɪ/ /əʊ/

Learn to Read

双元音由两个元音组成，发音时由一个元音向另一个元音滑动，口型有变化。前一个元音重、长、清晰，后一个元音轻、短、模糊。

/aɪ/	/baɪ/	/taɪm/	/faɪn/	/paɪ/	/saɪd/
/aʊ/	/naʊ/	/haʊs/	/praʊd/	/taʊn/	/daʊn/
/eɪ/	/keɪk/	/geɪm/	/leɪt/	/pleɪ/	/meɪk/
/əʊ/	/kəʊld/	/həʊm/	/kəʊt/	/nəʊz/	/nəʊ/

like /laɪk/　　　　fly /flaɪ/　　　　kite /kaɪt/
喜欢　　　　　　　飞　　　　　　　　风筝

I like to fly a kite.

cow /kaʊ/　　　　house /haʊs/　　　now /naʊ/
奶牛　　　　　　　房子　　　　　　　现在

The cow is in the house now.

轻松学语音

w**ai**t /weɪt/　　　　pl**a**ne /pleɪn/　　　　g**a**te /geɪt/
等待　　　　　　　　飞机　　　　　　　　门

Wait for the plane at Gate 8.

kn**ow** /nəʊ/　　　　c**oa**t /kəʊt/　　　　sh**ow** /ʃəʊ/
知道　　　　　　　　大衣　　　　　　　　表演

I know a coat show.

Dialogue

A: Take a bunch of flowers home for your wife, sir.

B: I haven't got a wife.

A: Then buy a bunch for your sweetheart.

B: I don't have a sweetheart, either.

A: Well then, buy a couple of bunches to celebrate your luck.

(A= a street vendor, B= a young man)

注释：A 是街上一个卖花小贩，B 是一个年轻人。这番对话是卖花小贩竭力向年轻人兜售花朵。他先提议让年轻人为家里的妻子买束花，被拒后又提议让年轻人为情人买。年轻人表示自己孤家寡人一个，没有妻子，也没有情人。再次被拒后，小贩语出惊人，言辞幽默："那么买两束花庆祝你的幸运吧！"

Passage

Grace lives in a small house in a big town. Behind the house, there is a small river. Around the house, there are flowers and trees. She is proud of having such a house. She likes to keep the house clean. She also keeps several goats and cows. She feeds them with grass and talks with them. They are her friends. Sometimes she goes out to do some shopping. At night she watches TV before going to bed. No doubt she enjoys living there, though she may feel lonely at times.

Unit 10 双元音 /aɪ/ /aʊ/ /eɪ/ /əʊ/

Tongue Twisters

1. Never say die! Try! Try! Try!
2. Sound in body, sound in mind.
3. Eighteen apes ate eighty cakes every day.
4. I don't know why Joan showed a yellow coat to the goat in the snow.
5. I know. You know. I know that you know. I know that you know that I know.
6. There is no need to light a night light on a light night like tonight, for a bright night light is just like a slight light.

译文：2. 有健康的身体才有健全的心智。5. 我知道。你知道。我知道你知道。我知道你知道我知道。6. 像今夜这样明亮的夜晚，就不需要点一盏夜灯，因为明亮的夜灯也会变得微弱。

Two Nature Rhymes

Rainbow at night,　　　　　　译文：傍晚出虹，
Is the traveler's delight;　　　　　　明日放晴；
Rainbow in the morning,　　　　　清晨出虹，
Travelers take warning.　　　　　　风雨送行。

Evening red and morning grey,　　傍晚天红早晨灰，
Send the traveler on his way;　　　旅者出门不后悔；
Evening grey and morning red,　　傍晚灰暗早晨红，
Bring the rain upon his head.　　　大雨淋头行匆匆。

轻松学语音

A Song: Do-Re-Mi

Doe, a deer, a female deer,　　　　译文：哆是一只小母鹿，
Ray, a drop of golden sun,　　　　　　　来是一缕金色阳光，
Me, a name I call myself,　　　　　　　咪是我叫我自己，
Far, a long, long way to run,　　　　　发是一条长跑道，
Sew, a needle pulling thread,　　　　　唆是一根针穿着线，
La, a note to follow sew,　　　　　　　啦是音符紧跟着唆，
Tea, a drink with jam and bread,　　　西是杯饮料加果酱和面包，
That will bring us back to doe.　　　 西将带我们回到哆。
Do re mi fa so la ti do so do!　　　　哆来咪发唆啦西哆唆哆！

Fun Time : Crossword（纵横字谜）

1	2	3	4
	5		

Down

1. on the river   2. used in questions   3. can   4. food

Across

1. a strong black animal   5. birds like to live in

44

Unit 11 双元音 /ɪə/ /eə/ /ɔɪ/ /ʊə/

Learn to Read

双元音	/aɪ/	/aʊ/	/eɪ/	/əʊ/
	/ɪə/	/eə/	/ɔɪ/	/ʊə/
/ɪə/	/nɪə(r)/	/hɪə(r)/	/dɪə(r)/	/bɪə(r)/	/aɪˈdɪə/
/eə/	/beə(r)/	/peə(r)/	/weə(r)/	/ʃeə(r)/	/keə(r)/
/ɔɪ/	/bɔɪ/	/tɔɪ/	/nɔɪz/	/vɔɪs/	/ɪnˈdʒɔɪ/
/ʊə/	/pʊə(r)/	/tʊə(r)/	/ʃʊə(r)/	/ˈflaʊə(r)/	/ɪnˈʃʊə(r)/

h**ear** /hɪə(r)/   b**eer** /bɪə(r)/   h**ere** /hɪə(r)/   d**ear** /dɪə(r)/
听说   啤酒   这儿   昂贵的

I hear the beer here is very dear.

sh**are** /ʃeə(r)/   p**ear** /peə(r)/   p**arent** /ˈpeərənt/
分享   梨   父亲；母亲

Share the pears with your parents.

45

轻松学语音

boy /bɔɪ/ 男孩   en**joy** /ɪnˈdʒɔɪ/ 喜欢   **t**oy /tɔɪ/ 玩具

The boy enjoys playing with the toys.

sure /ʃʊə(r)/ 肯定   **t**ourist /ˈtʊərɪst/ 游客   **p**oor /pʊə(r)/ 贫穷的

I'm not sure whether the tourist is rich or poor.

Dialogue 1

Roy: Would you like to have dinner with me tomorrow?

Joan: Sure. Where shall we go?

Roy: What about the Chinese restaurant down the street?

Joan: Good idea! I like their Beijing Roast Duck very much.

Roy: OK. Let's go there tomorrow.

Dialogue 2

Joan: The air here is fresh and the sky is clear.

Roy: But I do not share your idea.

Joan: I don't care whether you share or not.

Roy: I only think things here are very dear.

Joan: That's because the air here is very rare.

Roy: But I can't put up with the price here.

Unit 11 双元音 /ɪə/ /eə/ /ɔɪ/ /əʊ/ /eɪ/

Tongue Twisters

1. A spoiled boy destroyed a toy for joy.
2. Are you sure you can endure the long tour?
3. Hello, dear friends! Can you hear me clearly?
4. Look! The big bear is wearing a big pair of new shoes.
5. A noise annoys an oyster, but a noisy noise annoys an oyster more!
6. The man with fair hair dare not repair their chairs there because there is a bear there.

译文：5. 噪音让牡蛎很烦恼，而纷繁冗杂的噪音更让牡蛎心烦意乱。6. 那个金黄头发的人不敢去那里修理他们的椅子，因为那里有头熊。

A Poem: Who Has Seen the Wind?

by Christina Rossetti ——克里斯蒂娜·罗塞蒂《谁曾见过风》

Who has seen the wind? 译文：谁曾见过风？
Neither I nor you. 你我皆不曾。
But when the leaves hang trembling, 但看木叶舞枝头，
The wind is passing through. 便晓风穿过。

Who has seen the wind? 谁曾见过风？
Neither you nor I. 你我皆不曾。
But when the trees bow down their heads, 但看万木垂梢首，
The wind is passing by. 便晓风吹过。

轻松学语音

A Song: Auld Lang Syne

Should auld acquaintance be forgot, and never brought to mind? Should auld acquaintance be forgot, and days of auld lang syne? For auld lang syne, my dear, for auld lang syne, we'll take a cup of kindness yet, for auld lang syne.

And here's a hand, my trusty friend! And give us a hand of thine! We'll take a cup of kindness yet, for auld lang syne.

译文：

怎能忘记旧日朋友 / 心中能不怀想 / 旧日朋友岂能相忘 / 友谊地久天长

友谊万岁 / 友谊万岁 / 举杯痛饮 / 同声歌颂 / 友谊地久天长

我们往日情意相投 / 让我们紧握手 / 让我们来举杯畅饮 / 友谊地久天长

Fun Time

经典英文电影台词（节选）

1. I'm king of the world!

   我是世界之王！

   Titanic《泰坦尼克号》

2. There's no place like home.

   没有一个地方可以和家相提并论。

   The Wizard of Oz《绿野仙踪》

Unit 11 双元音 /ɪə/ /eə/ /ɔɪ/ /ʊə/ /əʊ/ /aɪ/ /eɪ/ /aʊ/

3. **Some people are worth melting for.**

   有些人值得我融化。

   Frozen 《冰雪奇缘》

4. **After all, tomorrow is another day!**

   毕竟，明天又是新的一天！

   Gone with the Wind 《乱世佳人》

5. **Of all the gin joints in all the towns in all the world, she walks into mine.**

   世界上有那么多的城镇，城镇中又有那么多的酒馆，而她却偏偏走进了我这家。

   Casablanca 《卡萨布兰卡》

6. **Mama always said life was like a box of chocolates. You never know what you're gonna get.**

   妈妈说生活就像一盒巧克力，你永远都不知道你会得到什么。

   Forrest Gump 《阿甘正传》

7. **Behind every successful man, there is a woman. And behind every unsuccessful man, there are two.**

   每个成功男人的背后，都有一个女人。每个不成功男人的背后，都有两个。

   Garfield 《加菲猫》

Unit 12　辅音音标 /θ/ /ð/ /j/ /ŋ/

Learn to Read

字母（组合）	th	th	y	n/ng
音标	/θ/	/ð/	/j/	/ŋ/

/θ/	/θriː/	/θɔːt/	/tiːθ/	/maʊθ/	/nɔːθ/
/ð/	/ðɪs/	/ðæt/	/wɪð/	/ðeɪ/	/ˈmʌðə(r)/
/j/	/jes/	/jɔː(r)/	/juː/	/ˈjeləʊ/	/ˈmjuːzɪk/
/ŋ/	/sɪŋ/	/θɪŋk/	/lɒŋ/	/sprɪŋ/	/ˈmɔːnɪŋ/

think /θɪŋk/　　　　**th**ick /θɪk/　　　　nor**th** /nɔːθ/
想　　　　　　　　　厚的　　　　　　　　北方

Think about the thick snow in the north.

this /ðɪs/　　　　**th**at /ðæt/　　　　fa**th**er /ˈfɑːðə(r)/
这　　　　　　　　　那　　　　　　　　　父亲

mo**th**er /ˈmʌðə(r)/　　　bro**th**er /ˈbrʌðə(r)/
母亲　　　　　　　　　　兄弟

This is my father. That is my mother / brother.

Unit 12 辅音音标 /θ/ /ð/ /j/ /ŋ/

you /juː/   **new** /njuː/   **yes** /jes/   **student** /ˈstjuːdnt/
你   新的   是   学生

—Are you new here? —Yes, I'm a new student.

young /jʌŋ/   **sing** /sɪŋ/   **long** /lɒŋ/   **song** /sɒŋ/
年轻的   唱   长的   歌曲

The young girl can sing a long song.

Dialogue

Hugh: Let's go shopping together. I need to buy a birthday present for my brother.

Alice: Oh, what do you want to buy? Have you got any good idea?

Hugh: No, not yet. He is now a first year student of middle school, so I'm thinking to buy him a computer.

Alice: Don't you think he is too young to have a computer?

Hugh: Oh, yes. What about a watch? It must be necessary to a student.

Alice: That's a good choice.

Passage

    Elizabeth enjoys doing many things. First of all, she likes cleaning, cooking and washing. She is quite good at cooking and repairing things. Secondly, she likes sports. She goes swimming in summer. And in winter, she goes skating and skiing. Thirdly, she likes reading and writing. In a word, she seldom sits there doing nothing.

轻松学语音

Tongue Twisters

1. Thick ticks think thin ticks are sick.

2. It is a fine thing to sing in spring, I think.

3. You broke the yellow yoyo young Hugh used to use.

4. Neither the father nor the mother likes this weather.

5. You can think of thin things, of six thin things. And I can think of six thin things, and of six thick things, too.

6. I thought a thought. But the thought I thought wasn't the thought I thought I thought.

译文： 6. 我有一种想法，但是我的这种想法不是我曾经想到的那种想法。

Two Rhymes

Walking walking, walking walking.

Hop hop hop, hop hop hop.

Running running running, running running running.

Now let's stop, now let's stop.

Are you sleeping? Are you sleeping?

Brother John? Brother John?

Morning bells are ringing. Morning bells are ringing.

Ding ding dong. Ding ding dong.

Unit 12　辅音音标 /θ/ /ð/ /j/ /ŋ/

A Song: Edelweiss

Edelweiss, edelweiss, every morning you greet me.
Small and white, clean and bright,
You look happy to meet me.
Blossom of snow, may you bloom and grow,
Bloom and grow forever.
Edelweiss, edelweiss, bless my homeland forever.

译文：

雪绒花，雪绒花，每天清晨欢迎我。小而白，洁而亮，见到我你面露喜色。雪白的花朵，愿你开放成长，永远开放成长。雪绒花，雪绒花，愿你永远保佑我的祖国。

Fun Time

1: A Policeman and a Thief

Policeman: I hope this is your last time. You know, I don't want to see you here again.
Thief: Why? Are you going to change your job?

警察和小偷

警察： 我希望这是最后一次逮住你了。你知道我不愿意再在这儿看见你。
小偷： 怎么？你要换工作了吗？

轻松学语音

2: Losing Weight

John: Tom's wife thought she was too fat and she rode a horse every day for a month.

Fred: So she got thinner a month later?

John: No, not she, but the horse lost 40kg.

减肥

约翰： 汤姆的太太认为自己太胖了，因此一个月来她每天都骑马。

弗莱德： 那么一个月后她瘦下来了没有？

约翰： 她倒没有瘦，马的体重却减轻了40千克。

3: Sleeping Pills

Nurse: Wake up! Wake up!

Patient: (startled from the sleep) Huh? What's the matter?

Nurse: I forgot to give you your sleeping pills!

安眠药

护士： 醒醒！醒醒！

病人： （从睡眠中惊醒）唔？什么事啊？

护士： 忘了给你吃安眠药了！

4: Kept Waiting Long

Waiter: Have I kept you waiting long?

Customer: No, but did you know that there are 3,479 rose patterns on your wallpaper?

久等了

服务员： 我让你久等了吧？

顾客： 没有。不过，你知道你们店里墙纸上的玫瑰花图案一共是3479个吗？

Unit 13 　辅音音标 /ʃ/ /ʒ/ /tʃ/ /dʒ/

Learn to Read

字母（组合）	sh	s	ch	j
音标	/ʃ/	/ʒ/	/tʃ/	/dʒ/
/ʃ/	/fɪʃ/	/ʃuː/	/ʃiːp/	/ʃɜːt/	/ʃɒp/
/ʒ/	/ˈpleʒə(r)/	/ˈmeʒə(r)/	/ˈleʒə(r)/	/ˈtelɪvɪʒn/
/tʃ/	/wɒtʃ/	/tʃeə(r)/	/ˈtiːtʃə(r)/	/lʌntʃ/	/rɪtʃ/
/dʒ/	/dʒʌmp/	/dʒɒb/	/lɑːdʒ/	/ˈbrɪndʒ/	/ɪnˈdʒɔɪ/

　　　　fish /fɪʃ/　　　　shop /ʃɒp/　　　　fresh /freʃ/
　　　　　鱼　　　　　　　商店　　　　　　　新鲜的

The fish in the shop is fresh.

　　　　television /ˈtelɪvɪʒn/　　　pleasure /ˈpleʒə(r)/
　　　　　　电视　　　　　　　　　　　愉快

Television gives me pleasure.

轻松学语音

child /tʃaɪld/
孩子

chicken /ˈtʃɪkɪn/
鸡肉

lunch /lʌntʃ/
午饭

The child had chicken for lunch.

orange /ˈɒrɪndʒ/
桔子

juice /dʒuːs/
果汁

jeep /dʒiːp/
吉普车

He likes to have orange juice in his jeep.

Dialogue

Jenny: What do you like to watch on TV, Charles?

Charles: I love quiz shows. What about you, Jenny?

Jenny: I like nature movies.

Charles: So do I. Do your mom and dad watch much TV?

Jenny: Not much. They're too busy. When they watch TV, they prefer the news.

Charles: Boring.

Passage

A panda looks like a little bear. It has black and white fur. It lives only in China, so it is called the national treasure of China and protected by the law. We can see pandas on TV or in the zoo. They look stupid and walk slowly, but they are lovely and everyone likes them. A panda is a lucky animal. The Chinese like it, and people of the world like it, too. Now there are China's pandas in many other countries, such as Japan and the USA. A panda isn't a common animal; it is bridge of friendship.

Unit 13　辅音音标 /ʃ/ /ʒ/ /tʃ/ /dʒ/

Tongue Twisters

1. Selfish shellfish.

2. Television gives me pleasure. Pleasure makes treasure.

3. Just now, a judge called Jack stood on the huge bridge.

4. "Shall I show you the shop for shoes and shirts?" Shirley said to Shelly.

5. If two witches would watch two watches, which witch would watch which watch?

6. She sells seashells by the seashore. The shells she sells are surely seashells. So if she sells shells on the seashore, I'm sure she sells seashore shells.

译文：1. 自私的水生有壳动物。5. 如果两个女巫看两只手表，哪个女巫会看哪只手表？ 6. 她在海岸卖贝壳，她卖的贝壳是真正的海贝壳。因此，若她在海岸上卖贝壳，我肯定她卖的是海岸贝壳。

A Rhyme: London Bridge Is Falling Down

London Bridge is falling down, falling down, falling down.

London Bridge is falling down, my fair lady.

Build it up with iron bars, iron bars, iron bars.

Build it up with iron bars, my fair lady.

译文：
　　伦敦桥要倒了，我美丽的淑女。用铁栏来建筑，我美丽的淑女。

轻松学语音

A Song: If You Are Happy

If you're happy and you know it, clap your hands (clap, clap).
If you're happy and you know it, clap your hands (clap, clap).
If you're happy and you know it, and you really want to show it,
If you're happy and you know it, clap your hands (clap, clap).
(stomp your feet / shout hurray / do all three)

译文：

如果感到幸福你就拍拍手，如果感到幸福你就拍拍手，如果感到幸福就快快拍拍手呀，看哪大家一齐拍拍手。

Fun Time

经典英文电影台词（节选）

1. I'll be back.

我会回来的。

The Terminator《终结者》

2. May the Force be with you.

愿力量与你同在。

Star Wars《星球大战》

3. To be or not to be, that's a question.

生存还是死亡，这是个问题。

Hamlet《哈姆雷特》

Unit 13 辅音音标 /ʃ/ /ʒ/ /tʃ/ /dʒ/

4. Love means never having to say you're sorry.

爱就是永远不必说对不起。

Love Story《爱情故事》

5. I'm just a girl, standing in front of a boy, asking him to love her.

我只是一个女生，站在一个男生面前，求他爱她。

Notting Hill《诺丁山》

6. A single idea from the human mind can build cities. An idea can transform the world and rewrite all the rules.

人类一个简单的念头可以创造城市。一个念头可以改变世界，重写一切规则。

Inception《盗梦空间》

7. Yesterday is history. Tomorrow is a mystery. But today is a gift. That is why it's called the present (the gift).

昨天是历史，明天是谜团，只有今天是天赐的礼物。所以今天才叫现在（礼物）。

Kung Fu Panda《功夫熊猫》

Unit 14　辅音音标 /tr/ /dr/ /ts/ /dz/

Learn to Read

字母组合		tr	dr	ts	ds
音标		/tr/	/dr/	/ts/	/dz/
/tr/	/triː/	/traɪ/	/treɪn/	/trɪp/	/strɒŋ/
/dr/	/drɔː/	/dres/	/drɪŋk/	/driːm/	/ˈdraɪvə(r)/
/ts/	/kæts/	/spɔːts/	/bəʊts/	/skɜːts/	/ʃɜːts/
/dz/	/bɜːdz/	/frendz/	/bedz/	/hændz/	/wɜːdz/

try /traɪ/　　　　**tr**ee /triː/　　　　s**tr**eet /striːt/
努力　　　　　　　　树　　　　　　　　　街道

Don't try to climb the tree in the street.

drink /drɪŋk/　　　**dr**ive /draɪv/　　　**dr**aw /drɔː/
喝　　　　　　　　　开车　　　　　　　　画

Don't drink and drive.

lo**ts** /lɒts/　　　　ca**ts** /kæts/　　　　boa**ts** /bəʊts/
许多　　　　　　　　猫　　　　　　　　　船

There are lots of cats on those boats.

Unit 14 辅音音标 /tr/ /dr/ /ts/ /dz/

birds /bɜːdz/   **frien**ds /frendz/   **han**ds /hændz/
鸟   朋友   手

Birds are our friends.

Dialogue

Audrey: There was another drink-drive accident yesterday.

Truman: How dreadful it is. Who is the driver?

Audrey: Tracy. Two children in the other car were on a trip.

Truman: Was it serious?

Audrey: Not really, only cuts to treat.

Truman: Thank goodness, no one was killed. It is dangerous to drive a car after drinking.

Audrey: Stop driving after drinking. I'll drive you home after I draw the dress.

Passage

Sandra is one of the college students. She enjoys listening to many kinds of lectures. When she has time, she would ask her friends to collect lecture notes. In that way, she saves time and avoids unnecessary jobs. She devotes most of her time to reading. What is more important, she never gets annoyed with learning new knowledge. She gets lots of rewards for her hard work. She is well-learned and can see things in their true nature.

Sandra has an aunt called Tracy. Sandra loves Tracy, and she visits her aunt on weekends. Tracy sells shirts and skirts. She likes to keep such pets as cats and dogs. She treats the cats very kindly. She tries very hard to train the dogs. She has some strange habits. She hates to travel by train, so she prefers to go on a trip by air.

Tongue Twisters

1. Trick or treat?
2. Edward's seeds are in that child's hands.
3. The truck driver is driving through the dry land.
4. Never trouble trouble until trouble troubles you!
5. The students often put their hands in their pockets.
6. The dude dropped in at the Dewdrop Inn for a drop of drink.

译文： 1. 想要恶作剧还是要招待我们？4. 麻烦没来找你，千万别自找麻烦。6. 花花公子走进露珠客栈要了一点儿饮料。dude /dju:d/, 花花公子。

A Poem: Dreams

by Langston Hughes　　——朗斯顿·休斯《梦想》

Hold fast to dreams	**译文：** 紧紧抓住梦想，
For if dreams die	梦想若是消亡，
Life is a broken-winged bird	生命就像鸟儿折了翅膀，
That cannot fly	再也不能飞翔。
Hold fast to dreams	紧紧抓住梦想，
For when dreams go	梦想若是消丧，
Life is a barren field	生命就像贫瘠的荒野，
Frozen with snow	雪覆冰封，万物不再生长。

Unit 14 辅音音标 /tr/ /dr/ /ts/ /dz/

A Song: We Wish You a Merry Christmas

We wish you a merry Christmas.

We wish you a merry Christmas.

We wish you a merry Christmas and a happy New Year!

Good tidings we bring to you and your kin.

Good tidings for Christmas and a happy New Year.

译文:

我们祝你圣诞快乐。我们祝你圣诞快乐。我们祝你圣诞和新年快乐。我们给你和亲人带来好消息。祝你圣诞和新年快乐。

Fun Time

1: I Couldn't Cry for Help

Victim: Oh, sir, a man robbed me of my gold watch a few minutes ago.
Policeman: Did you cry out for help?
Victim: No, I dare not. I have four gold teeth in my mouth!

我不能呼救

受害者：哦，先生，几分钟前一个人抢了我的金手表。
警察：你呼救了吗？
受害者：没有。我不敢呀，我嘴里还有四颗金牙呢！

2: Are Flies Yummy?

Tony and his father are eating dinner.
Suddenly Tony asks his father, "Dad, are flies yummy?"
Dad frowns and says, "No, I think it's yucky. Why do you ask me this question? It's a silly question."
But Tony says, "There was one fly in your plate."

苍蝇好吃吗？

托尼正和他爸爸一起吃晚餐。

突然，托尼问他的爸爸："爸爸，苍蝇好吃吗？"

爸爸皱眉说："我想不好吃。你怎么问这个问题？这可是个愚蠢的问题。"

可是托尼说："刚才你盘子里有一只苍蝇。"

3: A Letter to Santa Claus

It would soon be Christmas, and little Tom was writing a letter to Santa Claus.
"Dear Santa," he wrote, "I want a bike for me, a washing machine for my mother, a good temper for my father, and a very long sick leave for my teacher."

给圣诞老人的信

马上就是圣诞节了，小汤姆在给圣诞老人写信。

"亲爱的圣诞老人，"他写道，"我想给自己要一辆自行车，给我妈妈要一台洗衣机，给我爸爸要一副好脾气，给我的老师要一个长病假。"

Unit 15　语音知识

Learn to Read

48 个国际音标		
20 元音	短元音	/æ/ /e/ /ɪ/ /ɒ/ /ʌ/ /ʊ/ /ə/
	长元音	/iː/ /ɔː/ /ɜː/ /uː/ /ɑː/
	双元音	/aɪ/ /aʊ/ /eɪ/ /əʊ/ /ɪə/ /eə/ /ɔɪ/ /ʊə/
28 辅音	11 个清辅音	/p/ /t/ /k/ /f/ /θ/ /s/ /ʃ/ /tʃ/ /tr/ /ts/ /h/
	17 个浊辅音	/b/ /d/ /g/ /v/ /ð/ /z/ /ʒ/ /dʒ/ /dr/ /dz/ /m/ /n/ /ŋ/ /l/ /r/ /w/ /j/
10 对清浊对应的辅音		
清辅音		/p/ /t/ /k/ /f/ /θ/ /s/ /ʃ/ /tʃ/ /tr/ /ts/
浊辅音		/b/ /d/ /g/ /v/ /ð/ /z/ /ʒ/ /dʒ/ /dr/ /dz/

28个辅音

爆破音	/p/ /b/ /t/ /d/ /k/ /g/
鼻音	/m/ /n/ /ŋ/
摩擦音	/f/ /v/ /s/ /z/ /θ/ /ð/ /ʃ/ /ʒ/ /h/ /r/
破擦音	/ts/ /dz/ /tʃ/ /dʒ/ /tr/ /dr/
半元音	/w/ /j/
边音	/l/

Similar Sounds

/v/ /vest/ /faɪv/ /ˈveri/	/n/ /wɪn/ /θɪn/ /sɪn/
/w/ /west/ /waɪf/ /ˈwʌri/	/ŋ/ /wɪŋ/ /θɪŋ/ /sɪŋ/
/s/ /siː/ /sel/ /seɪm/	/s/ /sɪn/ /sɪŋ/ /sæŋk/
/ʃ/ /ʃiː/ /ʃel/ /ʃeɪm/	/θ/ /θɪn/ /θɪŋ/ /θæŋk/

/æ/	/aɪ/	/eɪ/	/æ/	/e/	/ɪə/	/eə/
/kæt/	/kaɪt/	/keɪt/	/pæn/	/pen/	/hɪə(r)/	/heə(r)/
/mæn/	/maɪn/	/meɪn/	/mæn/	/men/	/dɪə(r)/	/deə(r)/
/fæt/	/faɪt/	/feɪt/	/bæd/	/bed/	/bɪə(r)/	/beə(r)/
/bæk/	/baɪk/	/beɪk/	/ræt/	/red/	/klɪə(r)/	/kleə(r)/
/læk/	/laɪk/	/leɪk/	/sæd/	/set/	/tʃɪə(r)/	/tʃeə(r)/

Unit 15 语音知识

Tongue Twisters

1. Very well, very well, very well...

2. Few free fruit flies fly from flames.

3. Mr. See owned a saw and Mr. Soar owned a seesaw. Now See's saw sawed Soar's seesaw before Soar saw See.

4. A big black bug bit a big black bear and made the big black bear bleed blood.

5. Peter Piper picked a peck of pickled peppers. A peck of pickled peppers Peter Piper picked. If Peter Piper picked a peck of pickled peppers, where's the peck of pickled peppers Peter Piper picked?

译文：2. 没有几只果蝇从火焰中飞过去。3. 西先生有一个锯，萨先生有一个秋千。现在在萨先生看见西先生之前，西先生的锯锯断了萨先生的秋千。4. 一只大黑臭虫咬了一只大黑熊，使大黑熊流血了。5. 彼得·帕特挑选了一袋胡椒泡菜。彼得·帕特挑选的是一袋胡椒泡菜。如果彼得·帕特挑选了一袋胡椒泡菜，那么彼得·帕特挑选的那袋胡椒泡菜在哪儿？

A Rhyme: Clap Your Hands

Clap, clap, clap your hands

As slowly as you can.

Clap, clap, clap your hands

As quickly as you can.

※ Shake your hands / Roll your hands / Wiggle your fingers / Pound your fists

轻松学语音

A Song: Jingle Bells

Dashing through the snow in a one-horse open sleigh.

O'er the fields we go, laughing all the way.

Bells on bobtail ring, making spirits bright.

What fun it is to ride and sing a sleighing song tonight.

Jingle bells! Jingle bells! Jingle all the way!

Oh what fun it is to ride in a one-horse open sleigh!

Jingle bells! Jingle bells! Jingle all the way!

Oh what fun it is to ride in a one-horse open sleigh!

译文：

冲破大风雪，我们坐在雪橇上，快奔驰过田野，我们欢笑又歌唱。

马儿铃声响叮当，令人精神多欢畅，我们今晚滑雪真快乐，把滑雪歌儿唱。

叮叮当！叮叮当！铃儿响叮当！今晚滑雪多快乐，我们坐在雪橇上。

叮叮当！叮叮当！铃儿响叮当！今晚滑雪多快乐，我们坐在雪橇上。

Fun Time: The Lion King（狮子王）

Mufasa: Simba! Simba, I'm very disappointed in you.
Simba: I know.
Mufasa: You could have been killed. You deliberately（故意地）disobeyed me. And what's worse, you put Nala in danger.
Simba: I was just trying to be brave like you.

Unit 15　语音知识

Mufasa: I'm only brave when I have to be. Simba, being brave doesn't mean you go looking for trouble.

Simba: But you're not scared of anything.

Mufasa: I was today.

Simba: You were?

Mufasa: Yes, I thought I might lose you.

Simba: Ohh. I guess even kings get scared, huh?

Mufasa: Mm-hmm.

Simba: But you know what?

Mufasa: What?

Simba: I think those hyenas（土狼）were even scareder.

Mufasa: 'Cause nobody messes with（招惹）your dad! Come here, you!

Simba: Oh no! No... Errrgg...

Mufasa: Oh, come here... Hah! Gotcha!

Simba: Dad?

Mufasa: Hmm?

Simba: We're pals, right?

Mufasa: Right.

Simba: And we'll always be together, right?

Mufasa: Simba, let me tell you something that my father told me. Look at the stars. The great kings of the past look down on us from those stars.

Simba: Really?

Mufasa: Yes, Simba. So whenever you feel alone, just remember that those kings will always be there to guide you. And so will I.

轻松学语音

附录一：语音小常识

1. 音节

单词都是分解为一个个音节朗读。在英语中，音节是以元音为标准，一个元音可构成一个音节，所以通常意义上一个音节是由一个独立的元音或者一个元音加上一个或多个辅音构成。一般来说，辅音不响亮，不能构成音节，但英语辅音中有3个辅音 /m/，/n/，/l/，读音比较响亮，它们和辅音结合，也可构成音节，即成音节。成音节往往出现在词尾，一般是非重读音节，如：madam, bottom, garden, cousin, apple, table。

英语单词的音节有多有少。一个音节叫单音节，两个音节叫双音节，三个音节或以上叫多音节。划分音节的方法：元音是构成音节的主体，辅音是音节的分界线。两辅音之间不管有多少个元音，一般都是一个音节，如：bed, seat, beau-ty。两元音字母之间有一个辅音字母时，辅音字母归后一音节，如：stu-dent, la-bour。两元音字母之间有两个辅音字母时，一个辅音字母归前一音节，一个归后一音节，如：let-ter, win-ter。不能拆分的字母组合按字母组合划分音节，如：fa-ther, tea-cher。

2. 重音

英语的每个词，至少有一个音节读得特别重而清楚，而其他的音节则轻而含糊。读得重而清楚的音节，叫作单词重音，又叫重读音节。读得轻而含糊的音节，叫作非重读音节。在多音节中，除了有主重音外，还有可能有次重音或双重音。主重音在左上角，用 /ˈ/ 表示，次重音在左下方，用 /ˌ/ 表示，如在单词international /ˌɪntəˈnæʃnəl/ 中，主重音是 /ˈn/，次重音是 /ˌɪn/，其他部分为非重读音节。单音节词只有一个音节，重音自然就在该音节上，如book, hand。单音节词不需要标注重读符号。大部分双音节词重音都在第一个音节上，如study, listen等。多音节词重音一般在倒数第三个音节上，如beautiful, ability。

附录一：语音小常识

句子重音是指在句子中并非所有的单词都像单独读音时读得那么响亮，只有部分词重读，部分词不重读，轻重结合才有节奏感。通常情况下，实强虚弱，即在一个英语句子中实词一般重读，虚词一般弱读。实词包括名词、形容词、数词、实意动词、副词、否定词等，虚词包括冠词、介词、连词等。代词经常不重读，但是指示代词、名词性物主代词、反身代词、疑问代词常重读。介词、连词是双音节可重读。句中的中心词要重读。例如：

'Who are you 'talking to?

I 'saw it 'myself.

'This is 'not what I 'mean.

3. 节奏

英语是"重音节拍语言"，重音音节大致是以相同的间隔出现，即从一个重读音节到下一个重读音节的时长大致相等。重读音节之间可以出现任意数量的非重读音节，但所用的时间却大致相等。为了使重读音节更凸显，英语的重读音节通常被读得既重又长，非常完整，而非重读音节通常有约简，元音常常要短，有时甚至缺损、弱化，这种轻重、快慢、长短，构成了英语的节奏。例如：

'Twinkle, 'twinkle, 'little 'star,

'How I 'wonder 'what you 'are!

4. 意群

意群是指相邻的，在意义和语法结构上紧密联系、表达较完整意思的一组词语。意群在意思上相对完整，在语法上密切联系，不能再分。很短的句子只有一个意群，较长的句子可能有两个或更多的意群。在每个意群之后应稍作停顿，在同一意群的各个词之间不能停顿，必须一口气读完，以便整体意思不致中断，使人能完整地理解讲话人的意图和目的。

轻松学语音

Will you please / sing a song?

There are two windows / in the room.

I get up / at 7 o'clock / in the morning.

He said / that he would do better / in his English study.

5. 连读

在连贯地说话或朗读时，在同一个意群中，如果相邻的两个词前者以辅音结尾，后者以元音开头，就要自然地将辅音和元音相拼，构成一个音节，这就是连读。

连读时的音节一般不重读，只需顺其自然地一带而过，不可以加音，也不可以读得太重，如 not at all 这个短语，连读时听起来就像是一个单词。注意：连读只发生在句子中的同一个意群中，在两个意群之间即使有两个相邻的辅音和元音出现，也不可连读。

(1)"辅音 + 元音"型连读。

在同一个意群里，如果相邻两词中的前一个词是以辅音结尾，后一个词是以元音开头，就要将辅音与元音拼起来连读。例如：

pick‿it‿up / half‿an‿hour / Good‿afternoon!

Please take‿a look‿at‿it.

(2)"r / re+ 元音"型连读。

如果前一个词是以 r 或者 re 结尾，后一个词是以元音开头，这时的 r 或 re 不但要发 /r/，而且还要与后面的元音拼起来连读。例如：

for‿every people / far‿away / her‿own bag / a pair‿of shoes…

There‿are four‿eggs on the table.

I looked for‿it here‿and there.

6. 失去爆破

英语中有六个爆破音，分别为 /p/ /b/ /t/ /d/ /k/ /g/。这六个爆破音的任何两个相邻时，前者失去爆破，即只有口型没有声音。也就是说，发音器官在口腔中形成阻碍，并稍做停顿，做好要发出这个爆破音的准备，但不要发出音来。

(1) 这种情况常发生在一个单词中相邻的两个爆破音之间，或者两个单词中相邻的两个爆破音之间，比如 goodbye 中 /d/ 失去爆破，a big cat 中 /g/ 失去爆破，sit down 中 /t/ 失去爆破。

He has a ba(d) col(d) today.

You shoul(d) ta(k)e care of the children.

Gla(d) to meet you.

(2) 爆破音 /p/ /b/ /t/ /d/ /k/ /g/ 在 /m/ /n/ /l/ 的前面时失去爆破，例如：Goo(d) morning.　Goo(d) night.

7. 浊化

英语中有三对清浊相对的爆破音 /p/—/b/，/t/—/d/，/k/—/g/。在以 sp，st，sk 等开头的单词中，清辅音 /p/ /t/ /k/ 分别要发对应的浊辅音 /b/ /d/ /g/，比如单词 sport，speak，skirt，student，story 等。

8. 同化

同化是指一个音因为受了另外一个邻音的影响而发成了这两个音之外的第三个音。同化可以发生在同一个词、复合词内或者句子相邻词之间。如：Nice to meet you，其中，/ˈmiːtjuː/ 连读成 /ˈmiːtʃuː/。常见的同化有以下四种：

(1) /t/ + /j/ → /tʃ/。

例：last year　/ lɑːstʃɪə /；What about you? / ˈwɒt əbaʊtʃuː /。

(2) /d/ + /j/ → /dʒ/。

例：Did you see it? / dɪdʒuːˈsiːɪt /；Would you mind it? / wʊdʒuːˈmaɪndɪt /。

(3) /s/ + /j/ → /ʃ/。

例：this year / ðɪˈʃɪə /；God bless you. / ˈɡɒdˈbleʃu /。

(4) /z/ + /j/ → /ʒ/。

例：these years / ˈðiːˈʒɪəz /。

9. 语调

语调是英语语音的重要组成部分，基本语调包括升调和降调。

(1) 陈述句读降调。It is a cat.

(2) 一般疑问句读升调。Is it a cat?

(3) 特殊疑问句读降调。What is it?

(4) 选择疑问句，先升后降。Do you like red or blue?

(5) 反义疑问句，先降后升。It is a cat, isn't it?

(6) 感叹句读降调。What a lovely cat!

(7) 祈使句读降调。Come in, please!

附录二：常见字母（组合）的发音

a 读作：/æ/

bag 包；**a**pple 苹果；**c**at 猫；**b**ad 坏的；**d**ad 爸爸；**f**at 胖的

a, e, ea 读作：/e/

m**a**ny 许多；**a**ny 任何的；b**e**d 床；r**e**d 红色的；wh**e**n 什么时候；br**ea**d 面包；h**ea**d 头；r**ea**dy 准备好的；w**ea**ther 天气

a, e, i 读作：/ɪ/

or**a**nge 桔子；vill**a**ge 村庄；jack**e**t 夹克；b**e**gin 开始；m**i**lk 牛奶；sh**i**p 轮船

e, ea, ee, eo, ie 读作：/i:/

sh**e** 她；w**e** 我们；th**e**se 这些；tr**ee** 树；w**ee**k 星期；gr**ee**n 绿色的；r**ea**d 读；t**ea** 茶；**ea**sy 容易的；p**eo**ple 人们；bel**ie**ve 相信

a, o 读作：/ɒ/

wh**a**t 什么；w**a**tch 看；w**a**nt 想要；d**o**g 狗；st**o**p 停止

a, al, ar, au, aw, or, oar 读作：/ɔ:/

w**a**ter 水；t**al**k 说话；w**al**k 走；sm**al**l 小的；w**ar**m 温暖的；**au**tumn 秋天；bec**au**se 因为；l**aw** 法律；dr**aw** 画；h**or**se 马；sp**or**t 运动；bl**a**ckb**oar**d 黑板

o, u 读作：/ʌ/

m**o**ther 妈妈；br**o**ther 兄（弟）；c**o**me 来；s**o**me 一些；m**o**nkey 猴子；r**u**n 跑；

轻松学语音

s<u>u</u>n 太阳；b<u>u</u>s 公交车；<u>u</u>nder 在……下面；d<u>u</u>ck 鸭子

a, al, ar 读作：/ɑ:/

cl<u>a</u>ss 班级；f<u>a</u>ther 父亲；h<u>a</u>lf 一半；c<u>ar</u> 小汽车；st<u>ar</u> 星星；p<u>ar</u>k 公园；f<u>ar</u>m 农场

oo 读作：/ʊ/

g<u>oo</u>d 好的；f<u>oo</u>t 脚；l<u>oo</u>k 看；b<u>oo</u>k 书；c<u>oo</u>k 烹饪

o, oo, oe, u, ue 读作：/u:/

d<u>o</u> 做；t<u>o</u> 到；sch<u>oo</u>l 学校；m<u>oo</u>n 月亮；sh<u>oe</u> 鞋子；r<u>u</u>ler 尺子；bl<u>ue</u> 蓝色的

a, ar, e, er, o, or, u 读作：/ə/

Chin<u>a</u> 中国；breakf<u>a</u>st 早餐；doll<u>ar</u> 美元；simil<u>ar</u> 相似的；hundr<u>e</u>d 百；moth<u>er</u> 妈妈；sist<u>er</u> 姐妹；wint<u>er</u> 冬季；<u>o</u>'clock 点钟；policem<u>a</u>n 警察；col<u>or</u> 颜色；doct<u>or</u> 医生；aut<u>u</u>mn 秋天

ear, er, ir, or, ur 读作：/ɜ:/

<u>ear</u>ly 早；l<u>ear</u>n 学；h<u>er</u> 她；s<u>er</u>vice 服务；b<u>ir</u>d 小鸟；sk<u>ir</u>t 裙子；g<u>ir</u>l 女孩；w<u>or</u>k 工作；w<u>or</u>ker 工人；n<u>ur</u>se 护士；h<u>ur</u>t 伤害

a, ai, ay, eigh, ea, ey 读作：/eɪ/

n<u>a</u>me 名字；c<u>a</u>ke 蛋糕；r<u>ai</u>n 雨；tr<u>ai</u>n 火车；w<u>ai</u>t 等；s<u>ay</u> 说；pl<u>ay</u> 玩；tod<u>ay</u> 今天；w<u>ay</u> 道路；<u>eigh</u>t 八；gr<u>ea</u>t 极好的；h<u>ey</u> 嘿；ob<u>ey</u> 遵守

i, ie, igh, uy, y 读作：/aɪ/

n**i**ce 好的； l**i**ke 喜欢； k**i**nd 善良的； p**ie** 馅饼； l**ie** 谎言； d**ie** 死亡； h**igh** 高的； n**igh**t 夜晚； r**igh**t 对的； b**uy** 买； m**y** 我的； wh**y** 为什么

o, oa, ow 读作：/əʊ/

g**o** 去； n**o** 不； cl**o**se 关闭； h**o**me 家； r**oa**d 路； b**oa**t 小船； c**oa**t 上衣； sl**ow** 慢的； kn**ow** 知道； wind**ow** 窗户

ou, ow 读作：/aʊ/

h**ou**se 房子； ab**ou**t 大约； s**ou**th 南方； m**ou**ntain 大山； c**ow** 母牛； h**ow** 怎样； n**ow** 现在； d**ow**n 向下； fl**ow**er 花

ear, eer, ere 读作：/ɪə/

ear 耳朵； d**ear** 亲爱的； h**ear** 听见； n**ear** 附近； cl**ear** 清楚的； b**eer** 啤酒； ch**eer** 欢呼； h**ere** 这儿

air, are, ear, eir, ere 读作：/eə/

air 空气； h**air** 头发； ch**air** 椅子； sh**are** 分享； squ**are** 广场； b**ear** 熊； p**ear** 梨； th**eir** 他们的； th**ere** 那儿； wh**ere** 哪儿

oi, oy 读作：/ɔɪ/

j**oi**n 参加； n**oi**se 噪声； ch**oi**ce 选择； p**oi**nt 点； b**oy** 男孩； t**oy** 玩具； j**oy** 高兴； enj**oy** 享受

轻松学语音

oor, our, ure 读作：/ʊə/

poor 贫穷的；**tour** 旅游；**sure** 肯定的

f, fe, gh, ph 读作：/f/

fat 胖的；**foot** 脚；**life** 生活；**knife** 刀子；**laugh** 大笑；**elephant** 大象；**telephone** 电话；**photo** 照片

c, ch, ck, k 读作：/k/

cat 猫；**cry** 哭；**school** 学校；**Christmas** 圣诞节；**clock** 钟表；**duck** 鸭子；**black** 黑色的；**kite** 风筝；**sky** 天空

w, wh 读作：/w/

wait 等待；**way** 道路；**woman** 女人；**what** 什么；**where** 哪里；**which** 哪一个；**white** 白色的

h, wh 读作：/h/

hill 小山；**hello** 你好；**who** 谁；**whose** 谁的；**whom** 谁（who 的宾格）

th 读作：/θ/

three 三；**thank** 感谢；**month** 月；**thing** 东西；**throw** 扔

th 读作：/ð/

this 这；**those** 那些；**there** 那里；**with** 和……一起

qu 读作：/kw/

quick 快的；**quiet** 安静的；**queen** 女王；**quite** 很

附录二：常见字母（组合）的发音

n, ng　读作：/ŋ/

thi**n**k 想；tha**n**k 感谢；ba**n**k 银行；si**ng** 唱

sh　读作：/ʃ/

fi**sh** 鱼；**sh**oe 鞋子；Engli**sh** 英语；**sh**ort 短的；**sh**op 商店

ch, tch　读作：/tʃ/

lun**ch** 午饭；tea**ch** 教；ri**ch** 富裕的；wa**tch** 看；ca**tch** 抓住

j, dge, ge　读作：/dʒ/

job 工作；**j**ump 跳；**J**une 六月；lar**ge** 大的；oran**ge** 橘子；chan**ge** 改变；bri**dge** 桥；knowle**dge** 知识

tr　读作：/tr/

tree 树；**tr**y 试图；s**tr**eet 街道；**tr**ain 火车

dr　读作：/dr/

drink 喝；**dr**ess 连衣裙；**dr**ive 开；**dr**aw 画；**dr**eam 做梦

ts　读作：/ts/

studen**ts** 学生；coa**ts** 上衣；ca**ts** 猫；frui**ts** 水果

ds　读作：/dz/

be**ds** 床；frien**ds** 朋友；bir**ds** 小鸟；car**ds** 卡片

附录三：常用口语

After you. 您先。

Any day will do. 哪一天都行。

Anything else? 还要别的吗？

Are you free tomorrow? 你明天有空吗？

Are you sure? 你肯定吗？

As you wish. 随便你。

Allow me. 让我来。

Any message for me? 有我的留言吗？

Are you crazy? 你疯了吗？

Are you kidding? 你在开玩笑吧？

As soon as possible! 越快越好！

Be careful! 注意！

Be my guest. 请便、不客气。

Between us. 你知，我知。

Bless you! 祝福你！

Believe it or not! 信不信由你！

Be quiet! 安静点！

Big mouth! 多嘴者！

Bottoms up! 干杯(见底)！

Can I help you? 我能帮你吗？

Cheer up! 振作起来！

Come on, be reasonable. 嗨，你怎么不讲道理。

Control yourself! 克制一下！

Chances are slim. 机会很小。

Come on. 来吧(赶快)。

Count me in. 算上我。

Congratulations! 祝贺你！

Dinner is on me. 晚饭我请。

Do me a favor? 帮个忙，好吗？

Don't flatter me. 过奖了。

Don't give me that! 少来这套！

Don't mention it. 没关系，别客气。

Don't push me. 别逼我。

Drop me a line. 给我个信。

Do I have to? 非做不可吗？

Don't be silly. 别胡闹了。

Don't get me wrong. 别误会我。

Don't let me down. 别让我失望。

Don't move! 不许动！

Don't worry. 别担心。

Enjoy yourself! 祝你玩得开心！

Excuse me, sir. 先生，对不起。

附录三：常用口语

Far from it. 远非如此。
Follow me. 跟我来。

Feel better? 好点了吗？
Forget it! 休想（算了吧）！

Get serious. 严肃点。
Go ahead. 继续。
Go to hell! 去死吧！
Good luck! 祝你好运！

Give me a hand! 帮帮我！
Get down to business. 言归正传。
Good job! 做得好！
Guess what? 猜猜看？

Hang on! 抓紧（别挂电话）！
He is a smart boy. 他是个小机灵鬼。
He is my age. 他和我同岁。
Help me out. 帮帮我。
Here we are! 我们到了！
Hold on. 等一等。
How about eating out? 去外面吃饭怎样？
How's everything? 一切还好吧？

Have fun! 玩得开心！
He is just a child. 他只是个孩子。
He lacks courage. 他缺乏勇气。
Help yourself. 别客气。
Here you are. 给你。
Hope so. 希望如此。
How much? 多少钱？
How's it going? 怎么样？

I agree. 我同意。
I beg your pardon. 请你原谅。
I can't afford that! 我付不起！
I can't help it. 我情不自禁。
I don't care. 我不在乎。
I doubt it. 我怀疑。
I have a good idea! 我有一个好主意。
I have no idea. 我没有头绪。
I'll be back soon. 我马上回来。
I'll fix you up. 我会帮你打点的。
I'll see to it. 我会留意的。
I'll try my best. 我尽力而为。
I'm afraid I can't. 我恐怕不能。

I am all ears. 我洗耳恭听。
I beg your pardon? 请您再说一遍。
I can't follow you. 我不懂你说的。
I decline! 我拒绝！
I don't mean it. 我不是故意的。
If only I could fly. 要是我能飞就好了。
I have no choice. 我别无选择。
I just made it! 我做到了！
I'll be right there. 我马上就到。
I'll show you around! 我带你四处逛逛！
I'll see you at six. 我六点钟见你。
I lost my way. 我迷路了。
I'm bored to death. 我无聊死了。

81

轻松学语音

I'm crazy for you! 我为你疯狂！

I'm flattered. 过奖了。

I'm his fan. 我是他的影迷。

I'm in a hurry! 我在赶时间！

I'm not in a good mood. 我没有心情（做某事）。

I'm on your side. 我全力支持你。

I'm so scared. 我怕极了。

I quit! 我不干了！

Is it yours? 这是你的吗？

It can be a killer. 这是个伤脑筋的问题。

It doesn't make any differences. 没关系。

It is a deal! 一言为定！

It is a small world! 世界真是小！

It is not a big deal! 没什么了不起！

It seems all right. 看来这没问题。

It's a fine day. 今天是个好天。

It's her field. 这是她的本行。

It's up to you. 由你决定。

It's incredible. 难以置信！

I'm dying to see you. 我很想见你。

I'm full. 我饱了。

I'm home. 我回来了。

I'm lost. 我迷路了。

I'm on a diet. 我在节食。

I'm single. 我是单身。

I promise. 我保证。

I see. 我明白了。

Is that so? 是这样吗？

It doesn't work. 不管用。

I think so. 我也这么想。

It is a long story. 一言难尽。（说来话长。）

It is growing cool. 天气渐渐凉爽起来。

It really takes time. 这样太耽误时间了。

It sounds great! 听起来很不错。

It's against the law. 这是违法的。

It's nothing. 小事情；不足挂齿。

It's hard to say. 难说。

Just relax. 放松一下。

Just wonderful! 简直太棒了！

Just wait and see! 等着瞧！

Keep in touch. 保持联络。

Keep it up! 坚持下去！

Leave me alone. 别理我。

Let me see. 让我想想。

Let it go! 随它去！

Long time no see! 好久不见！

Make yourself at home! 就当在家一样！

My God! 天哪！

Me, too. 我也是。

My hands are full right now. 我现在很忙。

附录三：常用口语

My mouth is watering. 我要流口水了。

My treat. 我请客。

Never heard of it! 没听说过！

Never mind. 不要紧。

Never say die. It's a piece of cake. 别泄气，那只是小菜一碟。

Nice talking to you! 很高兴和你聊天！

No doubt about it! 勿庸置疑！

None of my business. 不关我事。

None of your business! 要你管？

No one knows. 没有人知道。

No problem! 没问题！

Not at all. 根本就不（用）。

Not bad. 还不错。

Nothing special. 没什么特别的。

Not yet. 还没。

No way! 不可能！（不行！）

Of course! 当然了！

Poor thing! 真可怜！

Right over there. 就在那里。

Same to you. 彼此彼此。

See you. 再见。

She is still mad at me. 她还在生我的气。

She looks blue today. 她今天很忧郁。

Shut up! 闭嘴！

Slow down! 慢点！

So do I. 我也一样。

So far, so good. 目前还不错。

So long. 再见。

Sooner or later. 迟早会的。

Speak louder, please. 说话请大声点儿。

Stay away from him. 别接近他。

Stay away from me! 离我远一点！

Still up? 还没睡呀？

Sure thing! 当然！

Take a seat! 请坐！

Take care! 保重！

Take it easy. 别紧张。

Tell me when! 随时奉陪！

That can't be. 不可能。

That's a good idea. 好主意。

That's all I need. 我就要这些。

That's all! 就这样！

That's neat. 这很好。

The answer is zero. 白忙了。

The same as usual! 一如既往！

This way. 这边请。

Thousand times no! 绝对办不到！

Time is money. 时间就是金钱。

 **轻松学语音**

Time is up. 时间快到了。

Try again. 再试试。

Wait and see. 等着瞧。

Well, it depends. 哦，这得看情况。

What about you? 你呢？

What a pity! 太遗憾了！

What brought you here? 什么风把你吹来了？

What happened to you? 你怎么了？

What's on your mind? 你在想什么？

What's up? 有什么事吗？

When are you leaving? 你什么时候走？

Who's calling? 是哪一位？

Who wants? 谁稀罕？

Why not? 好呀！(为什么不呢 ?)

Time will tell. 时间会证明的。

Watch out! 当心。

We're all for it. 我们全都同意。

What a good deal! 真便宜！

What a surprise! 太令人惊讶了！

Whatever you say! 随便你！

What's new? 最近如何？

What's the rush? 什么事那么匆忙？

What's your major? 你学什么专业？

Who knows! 天晓得！

Who told you that? 谁告诉你的？

Why are you so sure? 你怎么这样肯定？

Why so blue? 怎么这么垂头丧气？

You are just in time. 你来得正是时候。

You asked for it! 你自讨苦吃！

You can make it! 你能做到！

You did right. 你做得对。

You make me jump! 你吓了我一跳！

You owe me one. 你欠我一个人情。

You're welcome. 不客气。

You want a bet? 你想打赌吗？

You bet! 一定，当然！

You can't miss it. 你一定能找到的。

You have my word! 我保证！

You never know. 世事难料。

You're the boss! 听你的！

You set me up! 你出卖我！

附录四：格言谚语

A

1. A bird in the hand is worth two in the bush. 双鸟在林，不如一鸟在手。
2. Actions speak louder than words. 行动胜于言辞。
3. A fall into a pit, a gain in your wit. 吃一堑，长一智。
4. A friend in need is a friend indeed. 患难见真交。
5. A good beginning is half done. 好的开始是成功的一半。
6. A good book is your best friend. 好书如挚友。
7. A good medicine tastes bitter. 良药苦口。
8. A journey of a thousand miles begins with single step. 千里之行，始于足下。
9. A little knowledge is a dangerous thing. 一知半解，自欺欺人。
10. A little pot will soon be hot. 量小非君子。
11. All good things come to an end. 天下没有不散的筵席。
12. All is well that ends well. 结果好就一切都好。
13. All rivers run into the sea. 殊途同归。
14. All roads lead to Rome. 条条大路通罗马。
15. All that glitters is not gold. 闪光的不一定都是金子。
16. All things in their being are good for something. / Every man has his price. 天生我材必有用。
17. All work and no play makes Jack a dull boy. 只工作，不玩耍，聪明孩子也变傻。
18. A man has his hour, and a dog has his day. 人有称心时，狗有得意日。/ Every dog has his day. 凡人皆有得意日。
19. An apple a day keeps the doctor away. 一天一苹果，医生远离我。
20. A new broom sweeps clean. 新官上任三把火。
21. An eye for an eye and a tooth for a tooth. 以眼还眼，以牙还牙。
22. An hour in the morning is worth two in the evening. 一日之计在于晨。
23. A stitch in time saves nine. 小洞不补，大洞吃苦 / 亡羊补牢，贵在及时。
24. A young idler, an old beggar. 少壮不努力，老大徒伤悲。

B

25. Better late than never. 迟做总比不做好。

26. Blood is thicker than water. 血浓于水。

27. Business before pleasure. 先工作，后享乐。

C

28. Christmas comes but once a year. 圣诞一年只一度。

29. Constant dropping wears the stone. 滴水不绝可穿石。

D

30. Desire has no rest. 欲望无止境。

31. First time strangers, second time friends. 一回生，二回熟。

32. Do nothing by halves. / Never do things by halves. 凡事不可半途而废。

33. Do not put all your eggs in one basket. 别把所有的蛋都放在一个篮子里。

34. Do not teach fish to swim. 不要班门弄斧。

35. Don't cry over spilt milk. / It's no use crying over spilt milk. 覆水难收。

36. Don't put off till tomorrow what should be done today. 今日事今日毕。

37. Do what you say, say what you do. 做你说过的，说你能做的。

E

38. Early to bed, early to rise makes a man healthy, wealthy and wise. 早睡早起使人健康、富裕又聪明。

39. Easier said than done. 说时容易做时难。

40. East or west, home is best. 东好西好，不如家好。

41. Easy come, easy go. 来得容易去得快。

42. Every man has his faults. 金无足赤，人无完人。

43. Experience is the best teacher. 经验是最好的老师。

F

44. Failure is the mother of success. / Failure teaches success. 失败乃成功之母。

45. Faith will move mountains. 精诚所至，金石为开。

46. Faults are thick while love is thin. 一朝情义淡，样样不顺眼。

47. Follow your own course, and let people talk. 走自己的路，让别人说去吧。

G

48. God helps those who help themselves. 自助者，天助之。

49. Great minds think alike. 英雄所见略同。

附录四：格言谚语

H

50. Haste makes waste. / More haste, less speed.　欲速则不达。

51. Health is better than wealth.　健康胜于财富。

52. He laughs best who laughs last.　谁笑到最后，谁笑得最好。

53. He who helps others helps himself.　与人方便，自己方便。

I

54. If winter comes, can spring be far behind?　冬天到了，春天还会远吗？

55. It is never too late to learn. / Live and learn.　活到老，学到老。

56. It is never too late to mend.　亡羊补牢，为时未晚。

57. It never rains but it pours. / Misfortunes never come alone / single.　祸不单行。

J

58. Jack of all trades and master of none.　门门精通，样样稀松。

K

59. Kill two birds with one stone.　一箭双雕。

60. Kings have long arms.　普天之下，莫非王土。

61. Knowledge is power.　知识就是力量。

L

62. Learn to walk before you run.　先学走，再学跑。

63. Let sleeping dogs lie.　莫惹是生非。

64. Life is not all roses.　人生并不是康庄大道。

65. Like father, like son.　有其父必有其子。

66. Look before you leap.　三思而后行。

67. Love is blind.　爱情是盲目的。

68. Love me, love my dog.　爱屋及乌。

69. Love never dies.　爱情永不死。

M

70. Man is not made for defeat.　人不是为失败而生的。

71. Many hands make light work.　众人拾柴火焰高。

72. Money is not everything.　金钱不是万能的。

轻松学语音

N

73. Never judge by appearances. 切莫以貌取人。
74. Never say die. 永不气馁！
75. No news is good news. 没有消息就是好消息。
76. No pains, no gains. 不劳无获。
77. No road of flowers leads to glory. 没有一条通向光荣的道路是铺满鲜花的。
78. No root, no fruit. 无根就无果。
79. Nothing is impossible to a willing heart. 世上无难事，只怕有心人。
80. Nothing venture, nothing gain. 不入虎穴，焉得虎子。
81. Not to advance is to go back. 不进则退。
82. Now or never. 机不可失，时不再来。

O

83. Old friends and old wines are best. 陈酒味醇，老友情深。
84. Once bitten, twice shy. 一朝被蛇咬，十年怕井绳。
85. Out of office, out of danger. 无官一身轻。
86. Out of sight, out of mind. 眼不见，心不烦。

P

87. Penny wise and pound foolish. 小事聪明，大事糊涂。
88. Practice is the sole criterion of truth. 实践是检验真理的唯一标准。
89. Practice makes perfect. 熟能生巧。
90. Pride goes before fall. 骄者必败。
91. Promise is debt. 一诺千金。

R

92. Reading enriches the mind. 开卷有益。
93. Rome was not built in a day. 罗马不是一天建成的。

S

94. Seeing is believing. 眼见为实。
95. So many men, so many minds. 人心各不同。
96. Spare the rod and spoil the child. 闲了棍子，惯坏孩子。
97. Speech is silver, silence is gold. 雄辩是银，沉默是金。

附录四：格言谚语

98. Still waters run deep. 静水流深。
99. Strike while the iron is hot. 趁热打铁。

T

100. Tall trees catch much wind. 树大招风。
101. The early bird catches the worm. 早起的鸟儿有虫吃。
102. There is no end to learning. 学无止境。
103. There is no smoke without fire. 无风不起浪，事出必有因。
104. There is no such thing as a free lunch! 天下没有免费的午餐！
105. Think twice before acting. 三思而后行。
106. Time and tide wait for no man. 时间不等人。
107. Time flies! 光阴似箭！
108. Time is money. 一寸光阴一寸金。
109. Time tries all (things). 时间检验一切。
110. Too many cooks spoil the broth. 厨子多了烧坏汤。
111. Truth is the daughter of time. 真理是时间的女儿。
112. Two heads are better than one. 三个臭皮匠，顶个诸葛亮。

U

113. Union is strength. 团结就是力量。

W

114. Walls have ears. 隔墙有耳。
115. Whatever is worth doing at all is worth doing well. 凡是值得做的事，就值得做好。
116. When in Rome, do as the Romans do. 入乡随俗。
117. Where there is a will, there is a way. 有志者事竟成。
118. Where there is life, there is hope. 生命不息，希望长在。
119. Work makes the workman. 勤工出巧匠。

Y

120. You are only young once. 青春只有一次。
121. You cannot step twice into the same river. 你不能两次踏入同一条河流。

89

附录五：自我检测

一、根据所学内容，读出下列音标。(20 分)

/θ/ /ð/ /j/ /ŋ/ /tʃ/ /m/ /n/ /k/ /t/ /s/

/æ/ /iː/ /ɔː/ /ɜː/ /aɪ/ /aʊ/ /eɪ/ /əʊ/ /ɔɪ/ /ʊə/

二、拼一拼，读一读。(15 分)

/skɜːt/ /glɑːs/ /haʊs/ /pleɪ/ /pʊə(r)/ /traɪ/ /kæts/ /θɪŋk/ /ˈtiːtʃə(r)/ /ˈdrɪndʒ/

/hændz/ /ˈmʌðə(r)/ /ˈdɒktə(r)/ /fɪʃ/ /ˈjeləʊ/

三、读出下列句子。(25 分)

1. Love me, love my dog.

2. Do you like tea or coffee?

3. What will you like to do tonight?

4. There are some trees behind the house.

5. I don't know what you can get from the games.

四、朗读下面的短文。(40 分)

　　Grace lives in a small house in a big town. Around the house, there are flowers and trees. She is proud of having such a house. She likes to keep the house clean. She also keeps several goats and cows. She feeds them with grass and talks with them. They are her friends. Sometimes she goes out to do some shopping. At night she watches TV before going to bed. No doubt she enjoys living there, though she may feel lonely at times.

参考文献

[1] 陈枝英. 边玩边学. 外语教学与研究出版社，1986.

[2] 何刚. 创新大学英语. 华东师范大学出版社，2011.

[3] 胡海燕. 掌握英语发音. 世界图书出版公司，2003.

[4] 简庆闽，陆建平. 休闲英语（趣味小品与游戏）. 浙江大学出版社，1995.

[5] 马承. 中小学英语语音过关教材. 西藏人民出版社，2003.

[6] 谭伟民，林红. 英语歌曲与表演. 高等教育出版社，2008.

[7] 汪福祥，李孚生. 国际音标与语音. 外文出版社，2006.

[8] 辛瑞青，郭思含. 英语语音入门教程. 中国水利水电出版社，2015.

[9] 杨曾茂. 英语谚语荟萃. 金盾出版社，2003.

[10] 张珠穆. 英文儿歌经典. 江西文化音像出版社，1999.